Dogs, Cats & Expats

Advance reviews for *Dogs, Cats & Expats*

Are two cats too many? Are four cats too few? The answers to these and other universal questions—like how to finagle a free car wash in Mexico or how to make a compact car even more compact—can be found between the covers of this book. *Dogs, Cats & Expats* is sure to please even the grumpiest gringo. Don't read this book! Unless you want to laugh. Then by all means read this book! Mark Saunders offers you the unvarnished truth. Take him up on it!

David Temple, *FIVE TIMES LUCKY*

"A blend of hilarious introspection, candid truth, and sharp wit. Mark holds up the mirror for us to laugh at him, with him, and at our own curious lives. What a pleasure!"

Michael Hager, *TIMES OF CLOUDS & SUN*

"Mark Saunders is one of my favorite humorists and observers of our generation. As a longtime appreciator, I recommend his deeply human essays based on the unusual world he inhabits, a tangential life between Mexico and the U.S. For anyone who appreciates humor, honesty, and entertaining insight, time with Saunders is time well spent."

Jan Baross, *JOSE BUILDS A WOMAN*

If you want to know why Mark and his wife Arlene moved back to San Miguel permanently three times, and if you want to know how Mark gets along in Mexico knowing "*solamente tres palabras*" of Spanish, and if you want to know how they sleep in a queen bed with an eighty-five pound Standard Poodle named Duke, and if you like to laugh out loud while reading silently, I highly recommend his delightful and hilarious collection of essays, *Dogs, Cats & Expats*.

Lynda Schor, *DEARTH*

"From the very first essay, Mark's humor and eye for detail deliver a wallop. You will find yourself laughing like you haven't laughed in a very long time. Mark has the wry sense of a cartoonist and a gift for stringing together the profane with as much panache as the sacred. He writes about the challenges of adapting to life as a Gringo in Mexico using humor, sometimes, self-deprecating in such vivid detail that the reader can't help but want to hurry to the next page. His book, like his previous one, "Nobody Knows the Spanish I Speak," is like eating the richest desert without gaining a pound. Both of his books are gifts to the world. I cannot recommend them highly enough."

Gabrielle Brie, *TAP DANCING ON A HOT SKILLET*

"Mark Saunders's book of essays about living and traveling in Mexico called to me since I live and travel in Mexico as well and am always interested in other folks' adventures. From beginning to end I was chuckling, then chortling as

I devoured Mark's delicious essays. Fun, soulful, and completely delightful."

Marty Fraser, *DIVIDED BY FOUR*

"Whether Mark is writing about his gigantic, bed-hogging dog or his pathetically miniscule, cheap car, the tales are told with verve, immediacy, and surprise...and lots and lots of humor. And couldn't we all use a heaping dose of that these days?"

Cynthia Claus, *AN ORCHARD SARI: THE PERSONAL DIARY OF AN AMERICAN MOM IN 1960S INDIA*

"Make room on your bookshelf, next to *Nobody Knows the Spanish I Speak*, for the latest offering from Mark Saunders. Whether or not you have a dog and/or cat, and regardless of your status living north or south of the border, *Dogs, Cats & Expats* will bring you smiles, chuckles, and the occasional guffaw. Enjoy this delightfully entertaining collection of essays from San Miguel's answer to James Thurber. (What was the question?)"

Rhoda Draws, *EXPRESSIONS IN ENGLISH & EXPRESIONES EN ESPAÑOL*

"Mark speaks with the voice of a generous human being, as generous with the reader as with himself."

Geoff Hargreaves, *THE COLLECTOR AND THE BLIND GIRL*

Dogs, Cats & Expats

A Miscellany of Essays

Mark Saunders

Author of *Nobody Knows the Spanish I Speak*

knishbooks

San Miguel de Allende, Mexico

Knish Books
San Miguel de Allende, Mexico
knishbooks.com

Book design by Ray Rhamey

ISBN 978-1-7375155-0-0

Library of Congress Control Number: 2021913718

Contents

In Memory of Duke

The World's Happiest Dog

I am fond of pigs.
Dogs look up to us.
Cats look down on us.
Pigs treat us as equals.

Sir Winston Churchill

Acknowledgments

First, I want to thank my wife, Arlene Krasner, for visualizing our lives together as an ongoing adventure and for sticking with me over the years, in spite of the million times I forgot to put things back where they belong or the toilet seat down. Those who know us best know she's the funny one in our marriage, and she's also much smarter than I am.

I also want to thank my father, Charles Saunders, for teaching me the value of humor. He is the funniest person I know, and I am never quite sure what he'll say next. He's 97 and last year he tested positive for Covid-19. About a month later, he ran a fever. The independent-living facility where he lives sent him to the hospital. The infectious diseases doctor interviewed my father and, according to my brother, Michael, it went like this:

Doctor: "Have you ever smoked?"

Dad: "Never."

Doctor: "Do you drink?"

Dad: "Why, do you have anything on you?"

I want to thank the many old and new friends who helped to make this book happen, with a special note of appreciation to the following:

The Dog Parkers for embracing us during our time in southern Oregon and for building Duke's Deck: Alison Stevens, Bob Owen, Brooke Warrick, Bunny Owen, Dan Boyle, Dasja Dolan, Hans Zylstra, Janet London, John Staveley, Laura Giusta, Leonardo Newmark, Linda Zylstra, Lynn Faust, Richard Larson, Sue Kreul, Tom Lavine (for the many photos of our dog Duke), Wendy Nankervis—and, of course, all their lovable dogs. An extra tip of the hat (and I do wear a hat) to fellow dog lover Dan LaFond and his famous gluten-free pies (https://sillyzaks.com/).

The writers who encouraged me throughout the process of creating this book: Cindy Rogan, Cynthia Claus, David Temple, Frank Gaydos, Gabrielle Brie, Geoff Hargreaves, Jan Baross, Lynda Schor, Marty Fraser, and Michael Hager. Special appreciation to Molly Best Tinsley, a superlative writer, editor, and mentor. I encourage you to do a Google search for their books to discover compelling novels and intriguing memoirs.

Muchas gracias to Frances Dinolfo and Geoff Hargreaves for editing my usage of Spanish in select chapters.

My book designer Ray Rhamey. Whether designing the outside cover or inside contents, Ray is the consummate professional and knows what he's doing. He's a master at his craft, not to mention a fellow cartoonist and writer. Check him out: http://www.crrreative.com/

The San Miguel Literary Sala for its dedication in reminding us that literature is important in our lives.

Players Workshop for its support of *Diez Minutos,* San Miguel's popular international ten-minute play that Michael Hager and I started in 2013.

The San Miguel Playwrights' Group for keeping new works for the stage alive.

Molly Best Tinsley and Karetta Hubbard of Fuze Publishing for their encouragement and support over the last ten years.

And, finally, last but not least, many thanks to Mexico. You are a beautiful country with a rich heritage full of gracious and generous people. I consider myself fortunate to live here.

¡viva México!

Foreword: The Definition of Sanity

Albert Einstein, the greatest scientist of all time, said the definition of insanity was doing the same thing over and over and expecting different results. Or maybe it was the greatest American politician of all time, Benjamin Franklin, who said it. Perhaps it was Mark Twain, my favorite writer of all time, who coined the phrase.

It doesn't matter who said it, because each time my wife, Arlene Krasner, and I moved to San Miguel we didn't expect or even want different results. We wanted to repeat the same wonderful experience we had the last time. That's why we kept returning. Which, I guess, would make us sane, despite reports to the contrary.

Our first move to San Miguel lasted two years (2005-2007). Our second gave us five years (2011-2016). We returned to this wonderful town in the summer of 2020, and now hope to stay here for the duration, however long that is and whatever that means. When we moved here the first time, we didn't know a soul and could barely speak the language. Today, we know several souls and a handful of bodies yet still struggle with the language. Spoiler alert: I should be better at speaking Spanish. I was taught it in elementary school by nuns from Latin America, took one year of high school Spanish, and spent nine months on Puerto Rico, where I was stationed during an overseas tour in the U.S. Navy. The net result of all this exposure? In Spanish, I am able to exchange greetings, ask for directions, and count change, as well as recite the days of the week. That's pretty much the sum total of my Spanish as a second language capabilities. No surprise there. I still struggle with English as a first language.

Besides, it's most likely too late now to do anything about a foreign language. In the classic Christmas movie *It's a Wonderful Life*, an old guy on a porch yells at the much younger Jimmy Stewart and tells him to kiss Donna Reed; the exasperated old man blurts out that youth is wasted on the wrong people. In contrast, a foreign language at this point in my life is wasted on the old and that old person would be me. If I had a do-over with my early education, I would try to master at least one foreign language when mastering a different language was still possible. Then again, we rarely get do-overs in life. Comb-overs, yes; do-overs, not so much.

Moving back to San Miguel for the third time was a double do-over for us. Granted, San Miguel is a soft landing for those wishing to experience life in another country, but Mexico is still a foreign country. I wrote about our clumsy experiences during our initial two years in *Nobody Knows the Spanish I Speak*, a book that follows a narrative thread from the time we left Portland, Oregon, arrived in San Miguel de Allende, Mexico, and stayed for a while. The book relates our first two years living in another country and ends with our move back to the United States. Certainly, a lot happened during those two years: miscommunication out the ying-yang, near-death experiences on the highway, the occasional scorpion, speed bumps the size of small Kansas hills, music and fireworks at all hours of day and night, and, of course, those uninvited stomach guests known as parasites.

But that was then, this is now, and now we're living in Colonia Guadalupe, an artsy neighborhood full of colorful houses and wall murals. It's mostly level, with several small tiendas, including an organic market nearby. If we exit to the main street in our neighborhood and take a right, it's a brief ten-minute walk up a hill to the famous St. Michael the Archangel Parish Church (*La Parroquia*) in the historic *Centro* district. If instead of going right, we turn left, we're a five-minute walk to *Fábrica La Aurora*, a collection of impressive art galleries in a former textile factory. Guadalupe is a wonderful, close-in, and very walkable neighborhood. We like it. What's even better is we are renting and living modestly on our monthly Social Security payments.

Some of what I wrote about in my humorous memoir may be outdated. Times have changed. Since our first arrival here in 2005 until now, the roads have improved, and you no longer risk driving off the twisting mountainside between the cities of San Miguel and Celaya; the stores are more plentiful, and range from organic tiendas to supermarkets that can rival many of those in the U.S.; the restaurants are far better, with San Miguel fast becoming the culinary center of Mexico; public workers now use tractors instead of merely shovels to tear up a street; the architecture is still colonial, the parks still beautiful; and more younger families are moving here, thanks to today's internet-connected mobile workforce; we even have Uber. My humorous memoir of our first two years in this wonderful city is now more of a snapshot in time, a freeze frame, if you will, like a fossilized insect trapped in amber. All right, I'm stretching the truth a bit here: I'm not quite that old.

The essays in this volume are stand-alone and may be read in any order without substantial loss of plot or penalty for early withdrawal. But take your time. As the reader, feel free to jump around in the book. Read one or two, then set the book aside and do something more meaningful with your life. Take a nap. Save a cat. Run a marathon. Watch a marathon on the Turner Classics Movie channel. Then return and read more essays.

Any essay in this book about San Miguel is from the viewpoint of an expat, that would be me, and most of the challenges I faced are what could be classified as First World problems, such as where to find a good New York-style pizza or safely get a haircut during a pandemic. Plenty of books are available about what life is like for Mexicans in the 21st century or the history of this vast and fascinating country, and I encourage you to consider those books, if you are so inclined. Without going into details, let me simply say

Mexico is a truly amazing, resourceful country and her people are friendly and gracious. Although at this point in my life I suppose I am not very religious, I feel blessed to live here.

I had originally planned the first essay to be "The Pre-Memoir Memoir" and to have it serve as the prologue to my sequel. But, I soon realized there was no true sequel coming out of my computer keyboard. My first book was about a unique experience, the first time we had lived in another country, with all manner of cognitive and cultural dissonance attached. Since we are now living here full-time for the third time, I believe I am no longer allowed the cover of rookie mistakes. I still make them, of course. They're just no longer valid excuses.

The essays vary in length and were written over a period of time, stretching from the second time we lived in San Miguel until the moment I'm writing these words. Because the essays were written at different times, you might find, like a bad pastrami sandwich, I occasionally repeat myself. Although many of the events described take place in San Miguel, some occur in Oregon or elsewhere. The essays are largely about our experiences as expats living in Mexico ("The Miracle at the Car Wash"; "Still Spanglish After All these Years"), as well as about dogs ("Sleeping with the Big Dog"; "A Dingo Ate My Baby Ruth") and cats ("Good Cats, Bad Cats"). A few of the essays are comments on aging ("They Died with Their Fitbits on"; "Where Have All My Punchlines Gone?") or other personal reflections in my life

(“Free Rubber Chickens”; “A Run-in with the Amish”). In a weak moment, I turned over the writing of one essay to my stomach (“Holy Pozole”). Another organ, my brain, asked later what the hell I was thinking? In my defense, it seemed like a good idea at the time, like trying a ghost pepper on a dare.

All right, you, young man in the back of the room, with your hand up. Don’t bother to ask. I know the question already. Why did we ever leave San Miguel in the first place? Hmm. Good question. *[insert long pause for dramatic effect.]* Please leave your contact information with the door monitor and, when I know the answer, I’ll get in touch with you.

I hope you have as much fun reading these essays as I had writing them. And don’t forget: every time a bell rings a chicken gets his wings. *Vaya con nachos.*

Mark Saunders
San Miguel de Allende, Mexico, 2021

The Pre-Memoir Memoir

They say you always remember your first time. I have the distinct first memory of floating in my mother's womb, kicking and waiting to be born. I recall emerging from her body to bright lights, getting slapped, screaming on arrival. I remember my crib had a swirling carnival of circus animals above it. I pooped a lot. I recall the first time I stood upright, teetered for a few steps, and then fell back on my butt. My parents applauded as if I had just flown solo across the Atlantic. My first words were a bunch of gibberish, a cross between "mama" and "caca-sissy-boom-boom." My first birthday party was most noticeable for the number of adults in the room chain-smoking cigarettes. It was the early 1950s and the Marlboro Man was just as likely a doctor as a cowboy.

Of course, I remember no such events, at least not consciously. In fact, I can't recall much of my life before the age of seven. I probably ate my fair share of paste and occasionally wet the bed; two accomplishments considered neither precocious nor book-worthy.

Henry James encouraged writers to be one of those upon whom nothing is lost. Joseph Conrad piled on with his rule

claiming the task of a writer is to make readers see. But what about those of us who set out to write a memoir yet are equipped with faulty or incomplete memories, writers with recollection skills that are less Sherlockian and more like what popped out of Mrs. Malaprop's careless mouth?

Watch any Godzilla movie and you'll probably see someone looking away at the precise moment of debacle, unaware that the great monster of film lore is about to roast another metropolis. I am a kindred spirit to that unaware person, which makes writing a memoir especially challenging for me. I admire writers who can plunge the depths of their life like James Cameron in a submersible and bring up jewels. I splash around in the shallow end of the memory pool and call it a day.

Perhaps that's because other writers are better armed to wrestle with their past. James Thurber, for example, claimed a near-photographic memory and, even late in life, said he could recall the birthdays of his fellow students from elementary school. I can't recall what I had for breakfast this morning, but it probably included toast. Maybe.

Then, of course, there's Marcel Proust, the father of all memory writers who, after savoring not toast but a French cookie known as a madeleine, went on to write *Remembrance of Things Past*, a seven-volume novel loosely based on his love of pastry. That's an exaggeration, of course. His many volumes cover more than a sweet tooth.

I have my own cookie memory. During my senior year in high school, I lost twenty pounds to "make weight" for the wrestling season. My parents didn't know what to do with me because I was starving myself by sticking to a diet of five hundred calories a day, supplemented mostly by chocolate-flavored laxatives for dessert. Before long I was thinner than a metal coat hanger. My Swedish grandmother came to my rescue and made me a five-pound tin of butter cookies, knowing it was my favorite cookie; I ate them all in one day. My cookie memory is only a paragraph, not seven volumes, but that's my point.

Did I have a small stack of pancakes this morning? Perhaps eggs? Surely, it couldn't have been bacon. Nobody ever forgets bacon. Besides, I'd still be smelling bacon on my mustache.

Put another way, I write with the broad strokes of an Abstract Expressionist rather than the tiny dots of a Pointillist. As a *más o menos* kind of writer, I round up or round down without distinction and as the mood fits. I like to think of myself as a big-picture sort of writer. I may not reach for all the gusto I can get, but I grab for the Gestalt.

Which leads me to my "Uncle Teddy" episode.

I was eight, my sister was ten, and my brother was two. Whenever we visited relatives in the San Francisco Bay Area, we always stopped by to see Great Aunt Thelma, a feisty, tiny, bent-over old woman who drank far too much whiskey, read *The Police Gazette* with the conviction of reading the Bible, and lived in a quaint cottage, along a curved cobble-stoned path, behind a large house in Alameda surrounded by flowers and shrubs and trees. At least I think her house looked

like a cottage but now, after so many years, I'm not sure. I know she didn't live in a mobile home park or at The Ritz-Carleton.

At the time, Thelma lived with Teddy, her third husband, a retired Merchant Seaman confined mostly to bed. It seemed all he did was sleep. But to me, Teddy wasn't just an Old Salt collecting a Seaman's pension—he was a pirate. And to re-enforce his pirate status, Teddy wore a patch over one eye.

Every visit ended the same. Before we could leave, Aunt Thelma would ask us to "Come and see Uncle Teddy." My parents would remain behind in the living room with my brother, who was too young to join us in visiting Teddy. I imagined my parents chuckling to each other as my sister and I reluctantly followed the old woman, Hansel and Gretel-like, into the bedroom, a dark and smelly place. I can't recall exactly how dark and smelly, but still, it was creepy. Aunt Thelma would turn on the light by the bed, rouse her husband awake, roughly shaking him by the shoulders, and, using both of her hands, pry open his one good eye. "Look who's here to see you, Teddy," she'd tell him. "Look who's here to see you!" The groggy ex-sailor would mumble something and fall back to sleep.

After a brief pause, my great aunt would pull back the sheets and expose the naked decaying body of her third husband. She'd turn to my sister and say, bitterly, as if warning her to stay away from all men, "See what I ended up with?"

Now, any writer with a better knack for detail and a mind capable of remembering things past would be able to describe the exact perfume Aunt Thelma wore, by brand and fragrance, and would flash back to days gone by whenever catching a whiff of the same in streets or stores. If I were better at my job, I would instantly recall the color and weave of the bedroom carpet and could devote an entire chapter to discussing its texture, as well as its dark, blood-like spots. I could make you, the reader, inhale the thick stench that hovered in the closed-up room, see what long-forgotten TV show was flickering on the small black and white set topped with rabbit ears like a Mouseketeer hat.

The truth is, I can't even tell you which eye Uncle Teddy covered with a patch. To this day, I don't know for sure, but since Teddy wasn't a spider or a horseshoe crab, I can guess one of two eyes and have a fifty-fifty chance of getting it right. Sadly, I've never been good at remembering details or paying close attention to them. I suspect the only practical reason I still carry around a photo ID is so that I won't forget who I am or where I live.

The stories and essays in this collection take place long after my seventh birthday and are all true, except the ones that aren't. And at this point in my life, I'm not sure I can tell the difference. That's because, unlike James or Conrad or Proust or Thurber and so many other writers I respect and admire and envy, I have a mind like a steel sieve.

Now I remember. I skipped breakfast. It must have slipped my mind. I did have coffee, however. Two cups, cream, no sugar.

The Miracle at the Car Wash

My wife and I are both short. It's not as if we met and got married in The Shire, but we are below the American national average for height. Granted, I might be considered tall by East Timor standards, yet just about everywhere else in the world I pretty much fail the "you must be this tall to get on this ride" test. But—and, fair warning, here comes a hypothetical—what if this isn't my real body? What if, miracle of miracles, my body was switched at birth and somewhere on this planet a much taller version of *moi* was ducking under doorways and dunking basketballs? I could be my own doppelganger, only shorter.

I mention this not to complain about my genetic composition, although I certainly have a number of issues to raise with ancestors once I pass this earthly vale; instead, I want to explain why Arlene and I prefer owning smaller cars, subcompacts and the like. It's easy: We can comfortably fit in them. Plus, such vehicles tend to be cheaper to purchase and maintain, which are solid arguments to be made in their favor when shopping for your next vehicle. Unless, of course, you buy a Yugo, which we did back in the day. It was the cheapest new car available at the time in America and still over-priced. Don't get me started. What do you call a Yugo with a flat tire? Totaled. What's in every Yugo glove compartment? A bus schedule. What do you call passengers in a Yugo? Shock absorbers. What makes a Yugo go faster? A tow truck. The jokes write themselves, although I didn't write those particular jokes and they truly didn't write themselves. The jokes appear in Jason Vuic's book *The Yugo: The Rise and Fall of the Worst Car in History*, a book my father found in a thrift store and bought for me as a joke. Good one, Dad. You got me.

As an example of our fondness for smaller cars, during one of our trips back to the United States from Mexico to visit family and friends, we rented the most fuel-efficient and smallest car on the airport car lot, which seemed like a good idea at the time. We were not carrying much luggage, after all, and it was just for the two of us. We had no plans to ferry the Walton Family back and forth to a reunion.

So, how small was this car? I'm glad you asked. The following morning, I made three complete passes through the hotel parking lot, clicking the remote key constantly. No luck, no car. It was gone. Some football player probably carried it away under his arm. My first reaction was to wonder how I would explain to Arlene that our rental car had been stolen and our passports were still in the glove compartment. No matter how many times I played the conversation in my head, it always ended poorly. Such conversations always do.

Finally, the Spirit Animal of Parking Lots took pity on me and there it was, our tiny rental hidden between two motorized behemoths. It was Detroit's version of finding yourself between a rock and a hard place, or, in this case, between a Ford Expedition and a Chevrolet Tahoe. Apparently, the audio signal didn't work on my remote key and the small car was so deeply embedded inside this automotive tall-treed forest that I couldn't see its meek lights blinking for help.

The next morning, we drove two hours in the small, fuel-efficient rental from our hotel in Sacramento to a restaurant in Reno, where we met an old college friend for a delightfully long breakfast. On our way there, travelling east on highway 80, we had passed through a forest fire in the Sierra Nevada. As long as our leisurely breakfast took, however, it was not long enough to wait out the forest fire. On our return trip, crossing the Donner Pass Summit and heading west, we saw the fire was now raging more fully than before, and it was getting harder to see through the smoke. I was behind the wheel and straining to see the road ahead. That's when I realized a much bigger car does have its advantages. Somewhere between the towns of Colfax and Auburn, a bear dashed unexpectedly in front of our car. I was traveling at least 65 miles per hour, and the fire-crazed bear looked to be traveling even faster. From snout to tail, the bear was longer than our car was wide. For a split second, its head turned to look at me, just as I was staring at it through the windshield. I like to think we exchanged glances and shared the same thought: Oh, fuck.

Arlene screamed. I pulled the car to the right shoulder and slowed down, bumping up and down over gravel, and then returned as soon as I could to the highway. We absorbed what had just happened—as well as what had not—in silence for many miles. It wasn't until we were safely drinking in the hotel bar later that we realized how lucky we had been. I suspect, we were not the only ones rattled. In my imagination, I knew how the bear must have felt.

With smoke swirling through the woods, the bear made it to safety, sat on a log, still shaking and struggling to catch a breath, still unnerved by his near-death experience. A raccoon walked up to the bear, stared, shook his head in disbelief.

The agitated bear looked at the raccoon and spoke rapidly, "What the hell? Did you see it? Did you see what just happened? That car almost friggin' killed me."

"You didn't see it coming?" asked the raccoon.

"No. How could I? It was too small. And painted silver. Jesus, nobody can see silver."

"You got to look both ways before crossing, dude."

"Hey, don't judge me. If you want to help, give me a cigarette," said the bear, still visibly shaken.

"You're going to smoke in the middle of a forest fire?"

"Why not? I need to settle my nerves. Come on, give me a cig. You're a raccoon. I know you have 'em. You guys steal everything."

If I were a smoker, I would have been sitting on that log and puffing alongside the bear. It was a miracle we were all still alive, including Smokey. But I wanted to tell you about a different miracle, one that happened at a car wash in San Miguel. And, yes, we owned a small car at the time, a Nissan Versa.

The second time we lived in San Miguel, it was in a mixed-use neighborhood in the Colonia of San Antonio. Our location was convenient. We were near stores and restaurants and only a twenty-minute walk into *Centro*, the town's historic district. The best bakery in town was at one end of the street; at the other end was a popular hotel where public events were held. In-between, there were houses, as well as businesses. Standing in front of our house, in a single glance I could see a huge ceramic tile image of Our Lady of Guadalupe on a building wall and, across from her on the same side of the street, the painted image of the backside of a bikini-clad woman looking at the Pacific Ocean, her hot body promoting a seafood restaurant. There's room for both saints and sinners in this town. Best of all, I could walk to my choice of one of three car washes on the street.

Owning a car wash in San Miguel is job security. First, there is a low barrier of entry to the car washing business: all you need is water, rags, soap, and a ton of elbow grease. This is old school car washing at its finest; wrap-around brushes, rollers, and conveyor belts need not apply. Second, it's affordable. For the equivalent price of about $5 USD, customers get something more closely resembling an auto detailing job than simply a wash and wax quickie. And, finally, it's relentless. As soon as a car is washed, the dust returns and the clean vehicle is suddenly dirty again, ensuring a continuous business cycle based on the core principles of supply and demand. Dust on. Dust off. Dust back on. For a long time, I had simply given up and given in to the dust and not had my car washed, unless, of course, the rain took care of it for me. But one November day, not long after the end of the rainy season, I had decided to throw caution to the dust and spend a whole five dollars to get my small Nissan Versa washed. Hey, Big Spender.

Our two-story house was on Stirling Dickinson, a street that more than makes up for its relatively short length by being something of a well-known local drag strip. That may sound like a contradiction, but, welcome to Mexico. *De jure*, the street only has two lanes, one for each direction. *De facto*, it has as many as five. Drivers pass on the left and on the right and in the middle. Horses during the Charge of the Light Brigade had better odds of survival. Thus, on our street, cars and trucks and motorcycles would travel as slow as five miles per hour or as fast as fifty-five miles an hour, taking any fictional lane that suited their fancy.

Out of the three car washes on the street that day, I naturally selected the nearest one. It was literally across the street from our house. In fact, I could stand at our front gate, hurl a water balloon at the owner, and score a direct hit. I would never do that, of course, especially since the owner of the car wash was a friendly fixture in our neighborhood. I would always wave to him and he would always wave back. We had

been on cordial hand-waving terms for nearly a year. So, when I pulled my Versa into his car washing space to get it cleaned, he greeted me with a wide smile as if I were a long-lost friend. The return of the prodigal car. He said he would have my car ready in an hour. I nodded, said that would be perfect, and returned home to my upstairs office.

An hour later, someone rang the doorbell next to our gate. Sure enough, it was the car wash owner, but he wasn't smiling. Instead, he told me there was a problem and he needed to show me. As we crossed the street, I thought it was probably nothing to worry about, perhaps a few scratches on a door or one of his workers had spilled beer on the car's upholstery. All of which means I was not prepared for what I saw: the entire rear-end of my car had been smashed, parts dangled loosely, tail lights crushed, license plate demolished. It was by far the worst wash and wax job I had ever seen. Wax on. Wax off. Car wrecked. He apologized several times and said he would take care of it. He explained in limited English that after finishing my car, they were pulling it back out onto the street when a speeding truck driving far too fast for the street clipped my car's rear end.

In my limited Spanish, I said I didn't understand. So, he repeated the story. I understood what happened; I just didn't understand why it happened. I've seen them back out many cars from the well of their "shop" and they always had a young kid stopping traffic. He said they forgot to see if the street was clear this time but he quickly followed up and assured me he would take care of my car.

Stunned, once I made it back inside my house, I let go and ranted. I was furious. I told Arlene that instead of a five-dollar car washing expense, we were now going to have to pay five-thousand dollars to get our car fixed. Our small car just got even smaller. I paced furiously—and, yes, I am not proud to say but my potty mouth was unleashed in all its immeasurable glory. In the animated film *Inside Out*, a young girl must deal with her emotions. The emotion of anger was drawn as a human in the shape of a square box, a volcano erupting out of his scalp, and it was voiced by the irascible Lewis Black. I had five Lewis Black's inside my chest, all jumping up and down, all erupting and shouting obscenities in uncontrolled rage.

Arlene told me to calm down and go next door to see if David could help. Now, David was and still is my personal mentor in all things Mexican, he plays Virgil to my Dante. David was born in Mexico City, moved to the USA in his early 20s and joined the medical profession as a nurse; he's fluent in both Spanish and English and is not easily upset. Arlene was right: she usually is right, which over time has led me to utter many *mea culpas* and eat much crow. Truth be told, no matter how many times you eat crow, it never goes down well and leaves a bitter aftertaste. It always gets old.

David agreed to translate for me and the two of us crossed the street to the car wash. By then, the owner of the car wash was standing next to another man, who was tall and dressed in overalls. The owner introduced him to us as his cousin,

and said he worked in a body shop and had agreed to fix the damage. The man asked when I needed the car back. It was Wednesday. I needed my car back on Friday but I was not feeling overly generous, so I told David to tell him I needed it back tomorrow, Thursday, by noon. David spoke with the man and then told me the man said he'd have it fixed by noon. We shook hands.

Suddenly, the world was a happy place again. I could see clearly now, sunlight beamed, birds chirped, butterflies were free, hummingbirds flitted forward and backward in search of their next sugar high. I was ready to swagger across the street and return home to high-five Arlene and give her a confident thumbs-up. I got this. All's well that ends well, as they say.

Only, it hadn't ended yet. Before reaching my house, David turned to me and, in a somber tone, said, "Prepare to be disappointed." Riding high on one side of the street and shot down by the time I crossed it.

I fret by trade and all night long I fretted. I couldn't sleep. I tossed and turned and stared at the ceiling fan twirling above. I am a first-class idiot, I told myself. No, make that an economy-class idiot. I gave our only car away to some stranger I met for a few minutes, whose name I couldn't remember, and whose language I could barely speak. I could describe to the police the man's overalls but that was it. I had absolutely no clue as to what he looked like. No paperwork had exchanged hands. I had nothing provable or legal in my defense, with the possible exception of pleading insanity.

Mr. Green Jeans could deny ever meeting me or taking my car. As the long night wore on, I could hear the anguished cries of my poor little Versa as it was being viciously ripped apart in a hidden chop shop in the middle of the campo. Oh, the humanity. Oh, the machinery.

At eleven the next morning, someone rang at our front gate. I walked out and saw my car, with what looked to be a new rear-end, in a white paint that matched the rest of the car. The body shop cousin smiled broadly and handed me my keys.

I didn't pay a dime or a peso for the repair work. I didn't have to file an insurance claim or wait for an adjuster to show up and photograph the damage. I didn't have to argue for months after with an accounts payable clerk over reimbursement. The result? I wasn't out five-thousand dollars as I had feared. I wasn't even out the price of the car wash, which the owner gave me for free.

I call it the Miracle at the Car Wash (*El milagro en el lavado de coches*). But in truth, it was a double-miracle: he fixed my car at no cost to me, and he delivered it an hour earlier than scheduled.

And earlier never happens in Mexico.

A Higher Standard

Like any red-blooded, meat-eating, sports-obsessed male, I didn't want a poodle—the long or the short or the teacup. The breed was not on my Top Ten list of dogs. Or on my Top One Hundred list for that matter. But Arlene convinced me that owning a Standard Poodle would be a good thing. So, two years after our manly female Chow-Husky died, we acquired Cassie, a 45-pound female black Standard Poodle. Today, I consider the breed to be Nature's best kept secret.

And I am not alone.

Many dog owners have been in on this secret for a long time. In fact, the history of poodle ownership—Standards, Minis, Toys—is littered with famous names. John Steinbeck, as we all know, traveled around America with a Standard Poodle named Charley. Other writers who owned poodles include Charles Dickens, Victor Hugo, Thomas Mann, Gertrude Stein, Erma Bombeck, Neil Simon, and James Thurber. Many poodle owners will come as no surprise, from Josephine, the Empress of the French, to Marilyn Monroe to Mary Kay. Still, other owners, such as shirtless Vladimir Putin, are head-scratchers.

Knowing a natural-born people pleaser when they see one, Hollywood welcomed poodles of all sizes with open arms. The number of La La Land celebrities who owned, still own, and loved poodles is staggering. A partial list includes female stars such as Katharine Hepburn, Shirley Jones, Grace Kelly, Mary Tyler Moore, Ellen Degeneres, Barbra Streisand, and Debbie Reynolds, among others. Male celebrities, past and present, who had or have poodles include Bob Hope, Sammy Davis Jr., Jack Lemon, Kirk Douglas, Cary Grant, Mike Nichols, Robin Williams, and Vincent Price, to name but a few. Admittedly, a good number of the poodles pampered in Hollywood represent the smaller models but Standards appear to be well represented in the collection.

John Heisman, one of America's most popular college football coaches and the namesake of the coveted Heisman Trophy, had a small poodle named Woo, which was often found on the sidelines during games and in team photos. Oscar Hammerstein, the famous American composer of such works as "Oklahoma!," "The King and I," and "The Sound of Music," owned a black female Standard Poodle. Billie Holiday had her Standard Poodle cremated in her favorite mink coat.

It is said that Alexander Pope, the famous 18th century poet, was saved one night from a sure execution when his poodle stopped a break-in at his house. According to the story, which some people and a few dog breeds have questioned, one of Pope's servants had entered the house after hours with the intent to kill the poet. The dog threw himself

at the intruder and held the man by the throat, thus preventing both the murder of his master and a premature end to some rather famous rhymed couplets. Man's best friend doesn't get any more loyal than jumping at the chance to save poetry.

Standard Poodles are hardy and strong, and they like to pull. An Alaskan named John Suter ran a team of Standards in the Iditarod many years back, and they performed quite well. His first team to include poodles finished 38th out of 52 in a race where just finishing is considered a victory. At some point, the Iditarod folks changed the rules so that only "northern breeds" could compete and that was the end of that. I like to think the poodles were in the lead in the Iditarod until they hit that first saloon with a cheese spread and show tunes on the jukebox. They are smart dogs who know their priorities and stopped for a quick bite, which ran well into the evening.

It is thought the Standard Poodle breed originated not in France, as many believe, but from either Germany or Russia. Indeed, the word itself stems from the German word "pudel," for splashing about in water. It is also thought the Standard was the original breed from which smaller versions, the Mini and the Toy, say, were developed. By those who decide such things, a Standard Poodle is classified as any poodle over 15 inches in height. For competitive purposes, there are many other, more demanding requirements; the dogs, for example, must be shown in one of three clips: Puppy, English Saddle, Continental. Because we had no interest in either competing in dog shows or being publicly humiliated while walking a dog, we kept our Standards, both Cassie and Duke, in the Puppy cut, the simplest non-frou-frou style available.

Standard Poodles even served in the military during World War II under something called the Dogs for Defense Act. In early 1942, the Army had classified 32 official breeds as "war dogs," including the Standard Poodle, eventually limiting the list in 1943 to only 18 breeds, of which the Standard Poodle, again, was considered one of the brave ones, proving that in time of war they also serve who sit and bark. According to the official military manual on the effort, the Standard's special traits included its unusual ability to learn rapidly, good retention, patience, agility, versatility, courage, keen nose, and hearing. All traits confirmed through our time owning Standards. Not one to miss out on a public relations event, Hollywood stars donated their dogs to the war effort, from Greer Garson's poodle to Rudy Vallee's Doberman Pinscher.

When Sir Winston Churchill's much-loved poodle, a Mini named Rufus, was run over by a car and killed, a fan offered him one of her pure-bred English bulldogs. The breeder was appropriately thanked and politely told, "If Mr. Churchill has another dog, it will be a poodle again." I fully understand the sentiment, for having Cassie, our first Standard Poodle, ruined us for any other breed. Duke, our second Standard, sealed the deal.

Cassie was a 45-pound black Standard Poodle. We called her Cassiopeia when she was good and Cassandra when she

was bad, but most of the time she was just good ol' Cassie. Standard Poodles, by and large, are graceful creatures. They don't run so much as they gallop, like a well-trained circus horse. Cassie, on the other hand, was very much a girlie-girl and ran side-saddle. However, she ran with such enthusiasm that her butt would swing out ahead of the rest of her body, much like a gate swinging back and forth. Even her walk was something of a fashion statement and gave her the look of Charlie Chaplin in high heels. We called her walk "ditty-bopping" and it seemed to fit. She was, in the words of a Tom Robbins novel, skinny legs and all. When three neighborhood Chihuahuas got out of their house and we were walking Cassie, they attacked her legs. In the scene that ensued, Cassie watched curiously as the little dogs barked at her; she was like a tall tree surrounded by midget lumberjacks trying to saw her down. It was funny to watch even if Cassie failed to see the humor in it.

Cassie was small for a Standard, and since I'm never one to pass up a cheap joke, I usually introduced her as "Substandard." Our dog groomer back in the United States used to paint Cassie's nails. One time, as we walked with her along a busy street, some guy stuck his head out of his car and asked, "Are her nails painted?" "You bet," I said. "And next week she's getting a bikini wax."

Another time back in Portland, while Cassie and I were standing in front of a store waiting for Arlene, a rugged toothless man with tobacco breath and tattooed arms came over to pet our dog. The man looked up, smiled, and introduced himself as a commercial fisherman-lumberjack-roughneck man of all trades who had just returned from a stint working in Alaska.

"These are great dogs," he said, rubbing Cassie's head. "People think they're wimps. But they're tougher than shit, man. Don't know if you know this, but in England before they started fighting Pit Bulls, they used to fight these here Standard Poodles. Swear to God."

"I didn't know," I said.

But under my breath, I said to myself, and I don't believe a word of it. Poodles are too smart to work that hard for a bunch of smelly, leather-jacketed men soaked in cheap gin. And for what? A handful of biscuits and a pint of room temperature ale? I doubt it. However, I did know these dogs were not always the pampered creatures we see before us. Standard Poodles were working class dogs, water fowl retrievers, and even those goofy haircuts had a functional purpose: to give the dogs mobility in the water and, at the same time, keep them warm.

Cassie, although a direct descendant of water fowl retrievers, hated the rain and absolutely refused to pee or defecate whenever it was raining, or if she did, she had to find a dry spot of ground before she would do anything. She wouldn't do her business, as we politely liked to call it, if she heard any noises, such as another dog bark or a car honk or the leaves rustling in the wind. She was very fussy about such things. And that, in a nutshell, is what I consider to be one of the key differences between man and man's

best friend. When a man has got to go, he's got to go and it doesn't matter if it's a home bathroom, a bus station toilet, in bed, behind a tree, or in his pants.

The constant grooming is only one of the costs associated with owning this sweet dog breed, however. When Cassie was a year-old, she almost died. A thousand or so dollars later it was determined that she suffered from Addison's Disease, an adrenal gland failure. The adrenal glands, which sit in front of each kidney, are responsible for producing a lot of hormones, including adrenaline, estrogen, testosterone, cortisone, and aldosterone. Addison's Disease, simply put, is when the body does not produce enough cortisone and aldosterone; to compensate, it is treatable with regular injections and daily doses of cortisone. If not caught or treated in time, the dog or person dies. Whenever we mention that Cassie has Addison's Disease invariably the other person will chew on it for a few seconds and then ask: "Didn't President Kennedy suffer from Addison's?" And we would just as invariably give the same response: "Yes. We think Cassie caught it at prep school."

We loved this dog madly, dearly, and deeply but she was, to be blunt, a money pit, considering her regular medication, emergency visits, occasional surgeries, the overnight IVs, and constant grooming.

No matter the cost, she was worth it. Sadly, Cassie died in 2008. When she passed away, I thought of the words from the song "Mr. Bojangles," the dancer whose dog "up and died, he up and died... And after 20 years he still grieves."

Two years after Cassie left us, we acquired our second Standard, Duke.

A good dog is hard to find and even harder to lose. We found two and lost them in less than 20 years. And, yes, we still grieve.

Sleeping with the Big Dog

Owning a small dog has several advantages over the big dog. When you take a small dog out to do its business, you don't always need to pick up what's been left behind. That's because half the time you can't even find it. A big dog, on the other hand, leaves visible traces that can be seen by a Google Earth satellite.

A small dog eats less and needs smaller amounts of daily exercise. Small dog owners, unlike their big-dog-owner counterparts, rarely find themselves bundled up late at night in a driving rain walking their dog. An owner of a small dog can ignore his or her pet's late-night call of the wild with impunity. Whatever mess one finds in the morning is too small to lose any sleep over.

A small dog can be carried easily, without fear of the owner getting a hernia or dropping either groceries or car keys. When a small dog tugs on its leash, the master's arm doesn't pop out of its socket. And a small dog can fit on one's lap comfortably.

On the other hand, there are no human laps large enough for a truly big dog, and when a big dog sprawls out on the sofa, you often find you have nowhere left to sit but in an uncomfortable straight-back chair or on a cold floor.

The differences are many, and I could go on. But perhaps nowhere is the difference between the small dog and the big dog more noticeable or greater than in their respective sleeping arrangements.

Clearly, if we had kept Duke, our 85-pound male Standard Poodle, outside in a dog house (not going to happen) or in a garage (we didn't have one) or locked out of our bedroom (tried it, didn't work), we wouldn't have had to worry about sharing a bed with such a large animal. The truth is we don't mind spoiling our pets and have always granted them equal-opportunity access to our house, including all rooms and furniture. We never dressed up our pets in human clothes or set a place for them at the dinner table or had them photographed on Santa's lap. Still, they were always family.

In our defense and to set the proper context, Duke had his own bed, a large, cushy dog bed covered with his own special blankets, on the floor at the end of our bed. But the dog was no dummy. He knew the difference between a $39 Costco dog bed with some smelly blankets thrown on top for fake ambience and a thousand-dollar mattress with a box spring and comforter. Given a choice, he picked Mattress #2 every time.

Arlene and I are not what one might call big people. Thus, a queen-sized bed gives us more than enough room for sleeping, as long as there's no more than the two of us on

it at any one time. The sole exception was when Sadie, our cat, all seven pounds of her, joined us. But like most cats, she attached herself to only one of us, usually Arlene, and thus became a nightly extension of Arlene's body. When Sadie joined us in bed, the geometry barely shifted and we were mostly unaware of her presence.

Duke was another matter. When he jumped on our bed, we knew it immediately; shock waves were felt, radiating outward from wherever he landed like an earthquake triggering a tsunami. Once on the bed, he would try to create a comfortable space for himself—sometimes kicking or banging into us, stretching his long legs for more room—until either he gave up or we gave up and we all settled down.

One night I was sleeping on my back, when Duke jumped on our bed. Failing to reach the open space between his two owners, he landed in a sensitive region below my mid-section. I think you know the spot I'm talking about. While Duke curled up between us and went to sleep, I curled up into a fetal position and gasped for air.

"What's wrong?" Arlene asked, half-asleep herself.

"Duke stepped on me," I wheezed.

"So?"

"So. He. Stepped. On. My. Balls," I said between short puffs, opting for the direct vernacular usage over the more medically correct terminology of *testicles*, because, let's face it, at that moment a one-syllable description was pretty much all I could muster.

"So?" Arlene asked again.

And therein exists another chief contrast in life; not between a small and big dog but between the male and female human anatomy.

I don't know why women are referred to as the weaker sex because, as far as I know, there is no female equivalent to finding oneself so instantaneously immobilized. A strategically placed swift kick to the groin can bring a big man down, no matter how small the kicker, faster than you can say: "Ding, ding, ding." Whether it's a codpiece, a plate of armor in the front, a cup or a jockstrap, the history of male fashion has always included a nod to such frailty. The simple truth is that no man has balls of steel. They're more like those semi-soft dumplings you find in Matzo Ball soup.

Duke stepping on my boys happened only once and never happened again. I remained vigilant. I stayed alert and slept on my side.

Still the fact remained, at some point during the night, we could always count on Duke jumping into our bed. Usually, it was during the wee hours of the morning when he suspected, I suspect, that he knew we would be getting up for the day soon and were less likely to challenge his move.

He was also inclined to jump in bed, if either of us were to get up to go to the bathroom in the middle of the night or if Arlene and I started talking to each other, even in a low, hushed tone. I imagine he thought our sleep pattern was already broken, so all bets were off and why not go for it? Duke probably had at least three pages of rules describing when

it was justified for him to get into our bed without a formal invitation. The net result, once again, was that an entire night couldn't pass without Duke making at least one effort to sleep on our mattress.

In high-tech jargon, Arlene and I sleep like most people do in portrait-mode with our heads on pillows and our legs extending downward, toward the foot of the bed. Duke, unfortunately, slept landscape, which cut off our access rights to much of the bed. Put another way, the small humans slept north to south while the big dog favored east to west.

With a small dog, you might be able to give a slight kick and gently move it off the bed. No harm, no foul. Not with Duke. I had to physically lift him off, eighty-plus pounds of dead, snoring, comatose weight in the middle of the night. As a result, instead of doing a dead-lift, Arlene and I concluded it was much easier to just scrunch up into a tiny ball of human bone and muscle, hunker down, and wait for daylight. Our Duke doth murder sleep.

The wild card in all of this, of course, was noise. And since loud noises for unknown reasons at unpredictable hours are part of the San Miguel package, we often found ourselves dealing with a lot of wild cards in the middle of the night. Whether it was a series of small bombs exploding in our neighborhood or the bells of St. Anthony's ringing to acknowledge who-knows-what, Duke didn't wait to be asked. He immediately jumped on our bed, stood on our pillows and leaned into the headboard, pushing his body as far as he could against the wall as if he were made of ectoplasm.

According to an article in the paper, there's a new class of guard dog, named the "executive protection dog," that can cost a prospective owner north of $200,000 to purchase. It's usually a highly trained German Shepherd who's good with kids and bad news for the bad guys. Like a four-legged cross between Mel Gibson and Bruce Willis, the executive protection dog chewed his way through villains, snuffed out fires, sniffed out bombs, found lost children, and still had enough time over to play fetch with the family … all before dinner. Next to these guys, Lassie and Rin Tin Tin were slackers.

It is generally assumed, the best benefit of having a big dog, in spite of having to pick up after it or walk it at odd hours or constantly feed it or losing your spot to it on the sofa while trying to watch your favorite TV show, is the sense of security the big dog gives you, especially as you sleep at night.

Unfortunately, Duke was a lover and not a fighter. The only time he showed aggression was when he was around smaller dogs and that's only if the little dogs barked first. Many, if not most, dogs will bark, bare their teeth, and warn a stranger not to take another step. However, when a stranger came to our house, Duke barked and smiled broadly, with an expression that was almost giddy; his happy tail wagged like a spinning propeller. Instead of saying "Get out of here or I'll bite your head off," it's more likely he was saying, "Eeee-hawww!!! We have company. Let's party!" Simply put, Duke didn't even pretend to be a guard dog, let alone a fully-trained executive class variety that costs a quarter of a million bucks.

If masked intruders were to break into our house in the middle of the night, we hoped one of them would be carrying a barking little dog under his arm, because that's the only way Duke would have risen to the occasion. Otherwise, we expected El Dukerino to sleep through the night, like a slab of granite placed sideways on our bed. We wouldn't sleep but he would. And by morning all our belongings would be gone. We might be gone, too. Duke, on the other hand, would have enjoyed a good night's rest.

As I grow older, I have come to appreciate more and more the wisdom of the ages. The old maxims, aphorisms, and clichés, passed down from generation to generation, like fire or a family recipe for *chicken marbella*, are almost always correct. In the matter of our dog, Duke, and his sleeping arrangements, we long ago decided to let sleeping dogs lie.

A Dingo Ate My Baby Ruth

The screen opens dark. A long pause and then we hear soft human cries and moans and sniffles; the screen, still black. Within seconds a deep male voice commands attention over the darkness: "*Per istam sanctam unctionem*..." and the lights go up to show we're in an upscale suburban American house, more specifically a well-kept bedroom, now packed with mourners.

The camera pans the room, showing close ups of distraught faces. Women and men of all ages weep or stand speechless, full of grief, left with nothing more to say, all waiting for the inevitable.

Quickly the camera zooms in on a series of framed photos of a loving family of five and their dog. Then just photos of the dog. The camera pulls back to reveal the same dog, now lifeless, in the middle of a king-sized bed. A young girl sits alongside Dexter, for that is the dog's name, and strokes the dog affectionately.

The deep male human voice we heard comes from Father Hannah, local pastor and long-time family friend, who continues giving Dexter the sacrament of the Anointing of the Sick with Last Rites: "... *te dominus gratia spiritus sancti,*

ut a peccatis liberatum te salvet atque propitius alleviet." A tall altar boy swings a thurible, an incense burner suspended from chains. Several people make the sign of the cross as a line forms and mourners approach Dexter, touch his paws for one last time, kiss his forehead or his long nose.

A young boy pushes his way into the room and through the crowd to see what's going on. In one hand he holds a half-eaten hamburger. A young girl next to him turns, points to it, and asks: "What's that?" The young boy replies: "Bacon burger." "Smells yummy," says the girl. The boy answers, "It is. Want a bite?"

Suddenly, Dexter's head snaps up. He sniffs the air several times and looks over in the direction of the kid with the hamburger. Dexter begins to drool.

The mourners shake their heads in disbelief, murmur to each other, now relieved. The confident priest nods his approval as if he never doubted the outcome, even though he was there to administer Last Rites. An elderly woman in the room clutching rosary beads looks to the ceiling and shouts: "It's a miracle!"

No. It's bacon.

I wanted to open with that fake scene from a non-movie for two reasons. The first is to show how, for many of us, our dogs are family and our love for them is unconditional. The second is to acknowledge that when it comes to bacon, the canine species is all in. So am I.

At this point, fair disclosure laws require me to mention there are no dingoes in this chapter and the only Baby Ruth candy bar is in the title. Still, I wanted to talk about the dogs of San Miguel—my dogs as well as other dogs—and what better way to draw the reader in than with a wretched pun in the title and the false promise of candy.

When my wife and I lived in San Miguel the first time, from 2005 through 2007, our dog Cassie, a black 45-pound female Standard Poodle, was with us, a breed of dog I now consider Nature's best kept secret. Standard Poodles are hardy and strong, and like to pull things, heavy things, not just pranks.

As an 85-pound, apricot-colored (some might say, San Miguel dust-colored) male, Duke was the opposite of Cassie and stood out from the colorful buildings and blue skies, not just the pack. He was a free-to-good-home dog we picked up from a family in Oregon who could no longer keep him. Their loss was our gain and Duke became something of an icon of oddity in San Miguel. Even people we didn't know who were twice removed from people we did know, knew Duke by name. One festive weekend in San Miguel, a group of nuns jumped out of their van and took turns taking their picture with Duke. Such photo ops happened all the time when we walked Duke. Strangers invariably waved us out of the frame before taking their pictures. They could easily explain the photogenic dog in their family photo album but would be hard-pressed to justify two aging gringos.

When we first lived in San Miguel the dog situation bordered on chaotic. Packs of dogs could be seen roaming *Salida de Celaya*, a wide, flat street that runs north and south

from the center of town. The only thing missing from these dogs were leather jackets with "Jets" or "Sharks" embroidered on the back and a few Sondheim lyrics barking out of the corners of their curled lips. During our second tenure in San Miguel, unleashed dog sightings were the exception and no longer the rule. That was due largely—if not entirely—to the efforts of civic-minded, dog-loving Mexicans and expats who would spend their time and money rescuing street dogs. I did not expect to find so many dog lovers in the middle of another country. But there I was and there they were.

The volunteer organization Save a Mexican Mutt, for instance, saved many a mutt's butt, exactly 680 over 12 years, but the rescue service closed its doors in 2015. Other organizations, such as the S.P.A. (*The Sociedad Protectora de Animales*) and Rescue San Miguel, continue to save abandoned street dogs, get them checked out by a vet, and, when the dogs are ready for placement, find homes for them, sometimes locally but often in the United States or Canada.

Still other dog lovers follow a less-organized, more ad hoc rescue approach. One February morning, an American woman stopped us on our street to tell us she and her friends had rescued a stray recently and one of her friends took the dog back home with her to Minnesota. I can only imagine the poor dog's confusion.

Stray Dog: "Hey, Lady, thanks for rescuing me. Last week I was rolling on the ground in 70-degree weather in the middle of Mexico with not a care in the world. Now I'm freezing my tukus off. Don't worry about getting me fixed. My boys just dropped, hit the frozen ground, and shattered into a million pieces. I'm good to go."

The town has several excellent veterinarians and most of them make house calls. The wild card in all of this, of course, is the noise factor. And since loud noises for unknown reasons at unpredictable hours are part of the San Miguel package, we found ourselves dealing with a lot of wild cards in the middle of the night. Whether it was a series of small bombs exploding on our street or the nearby bells of St. Anthony's ringing to acknowledge who-knows-what or a powerful summer thunderstorm rolling through, Duke didn't even wait to be asked. He immediately jumped on our bed, stood on our pillows and leaned into the headboard. It was painful to watch.

Dogs are everywhere in San Miguel and they come in all breeds, shapes, weights, colors, sizes, and temperaments. Perhaps the most common breed of street dog is what collectively can be called "The San Miguel Special." It's a small, dusty-white dog with knotted fur, something of a cross between a lot of dogs and a lot of other dogs. If a typical street dog took a DNA test from Ancestry.com, it would come as little surprise that the dog had many branches. Fortunately for dogs, a family tree has more than one use.

During my years in San Miguel, I kept a Mexico survival kit with me at all times. The kit included an Imodium D tablet for stomach distress, a Benadryl tablet for scorpion

distress, and a dog pickup bag for pet distress. One day I was walking alone, without Duke, and traveling away from *Centro* heading south on *Zacateros*, a two-way street dotted with small restaurants and even smaller shops. I noticed an expat couple, about my age, also moving south and walking their dog on the opposite side of the street. The man was first in line and the woman followed, with their leashed dog, a mid-sized mixed-breed creature, walking between them. The dog stopped on the sidewalk to do what is commonly referred to ex-Navy men such as myself as a dump. The woman said something to the man, who glanced back, saw what his dog was doing, and picked up his pace, trying to get as far away from the dog and his wife as quickly as possible. The woman, stuck doing the dirty work, as is so often the case in the History of Man, opened her purse and took out a flimsy piece of tissue paper. She knelt down.

Responding to the John Williams-inspired film score in my head, I dashed across the street and said, "Ma-am, don't use that." I pulled out a plastic dog waste bag from my back pocket. "Use this," I said, handing her the bag. She looked up at me with gratitude, her eyes fluttering, as if to say, "Thank you, Super Dog Poop Man." When she stood, she reached over with her free hand, grabbed my cheek, tugged it gently and said, with a Southern drawl, "You're such a sweet thang." Honestly, my cheek had not been pulled in that way since I was ten.

And that's another thing I appreciate about living in San Miguel. No matter how old you are, the town always finds ways to make you feel younger. Even in dog years.

Bandit and the Bunny Slippers

Celebrated Scottish poet Robert Burns, in his famous poem "To A Louse, On Seeing One on a Lady's Bonnet at Church," reminded us of the difference between how we see ourselves and how others see us. The importance and value of honest self-reflection, to put it another way. Bandit, I am sure, would have disagreed with Sir Robert.

Bandit was our 105-pound female dog, a Chow-Husky mix; she saw herself as a wee lass of a lapdog, to keep with the Scottish slant. Most likely, she would have eaten the bug instead of converting it to a metaphor. After a good Oregon soak, we would take Bandit for a walk and she would eat worms crawling on the pavement. We were not ones to criticize Bandit in her choice of snacks; after all, we've been known to spend $25 for a small plate of snails in a French restaurant.

Bandit lived with us, along with two cats, in the first house we had purchased in Portland, Oregon, a three-bedroom, one-bath 1940s ranch, with a double-lot backyard full of mature growth, a fantastic tree house, and bugs. The interior had a cabin-like feel, with an overabundance of wood and, as we found out much later to our disappointment,

carpenter ants, an insect profession I knew nothing about until moving to forest country. Because the house had green carpet and its windows were partly obscured by shrubs and trees, Arlene said she felt as if she were living in a tree. No matter where Arlene sat in the house, Bandit always tried to get in her lap.

We acquired this dog in an odd roundabout way. While visiting my brother, Michael, in San Jose, a woman frantically knocked on his door asking for help. Apparently, her friend was my brother's neighbor and he owned Bandit at the time. The man had passed out from snorting some kind of powder. We rushed over, helped to revive him, then called 9-1-1. Meanwhile, his girlfriend went into the bathroom and finished snorting whatever was on the counter, even though it had just caused her friend to overdose. The mind boggled and another Darwin Award candidate emerged from the crowd, a clear front-runner.

As a result, Michael inherited Bandit. A few years later, my brother could no longer keep Bandit, so he gave her to my parents, who already had a small Westie white terrier named Precious. At some point, my parents moved from Sacramento to the Portland area, bringing their two dogs with them. The two dogs had mastered a circus act. Bandit would stick her snout under Precious and flip the tiny dog in the air, something of her own version of dwarf tossing. After each flip, Bandit would smile proudly and wag her tail.

About a year later, my parents returned to Sacramento, leaving Bandit with us. We suspected it had always been their plan to unload the big hairy dog on us and wanted to stay for a year to make it look good and make us less suspicious of their intention.

Every afternoon, around three, Bandit would get up from her bed on our porch and waddle down the street. It was a dead-end street with very little traffic, and only seven houses on either side. She would always stop by the same neighbor's house for a dog treat and a brief visit. Then, she'd waddle back up and would be waiting for us when we returned home from work. We had tried keeping Bandit in the house but she had abandonment issues and liked to chew. For a while we kept her in the backyard, which was fenced. Unfortunately, she had a habit of sticking her nose inside the cat door to see what was going on in the house. The cats would assume the cartoon roles of Tom and Jerry and take turns swatting her intruding nose, like a punching bag. Finally, we concluded it was safer and perhaps wiser to allow Bandit to sit outside on our front porch. The stocky Chow breed is powerful and protective, and guarding the front door gave Bandit something to do. She had plenty of water, a soft bed, some treats, and no cats.

This was the Pacific Northwest. I suspected of the nearly 15 houses on our street, ours was the only one without a firearm. Even though most or all of our neighbors had weapons and ammo, they were still afraid of the gun-crazed lunatic directly across the street from our house. It was well-known that Gun Guy kept a loaded weapon in his car's glove compartment. He was a primary fixture in pro-gun rallies

around town and even sat in the front row of a local news show about the Second Amendment, loudly screaming his opinion to the camera. When his dog became ill, we were told he shot the dog and buried it in his backyard.

With so little in common, we rarely interacted with Gun Guy, and he mostly kept to himself, which was unusual for the neighborhood. It was the sort of street where people would party together, either in each other's homes or yards; they'd play cards, as well as share lawnmowers, kitchen supplies, and recipes. On the Fourth of July, for instance, we always had a street celebration, with someone in charge of fireworks. Unlike every other dog we've had, Bandit didn't care about the noise fireworks made. On the contrary, she would run into the middle of the street and bark at the spinning fireworks. When done, she'd stroll back to the sidewalk, her thick dog hair smoldering like a supporting actor's outfit in the movie *Backdraft*.

During our first September in our first house, a log truck turned into our street and unloaded a pile of logs in front of a neighbor's house, at the far end of the street. The owner spent his evenings cutting up the logs for firewood. I was so impressed I went out and bought plaid shirts for the winter. The man clearly knew his way around trees. A couple of years earlier, according to a story related to me by another neighbor, Log Guy wanted to top the tall birchwood trees in his backyard. He was going to need someone to assist and help guide the cut trees safely to the ground, and the only man available or willing that Saturday afternoon was Gun Guy.

Gun Guy was about my size, which means he didn't fit the typical brawny logger profile, but, to his credit, he agreed to help. Log Guy gave him one end of rope and said all he had to do was stand across the street, hold the rope and use it to keep the cut tree in place and guide it safely to the ground, ensuring it didn't slam into the house or another neighbor's yard. But first, Log Guy would climb the tree and trim the top, removing about a third of the tree. After making the cut, he planned to rush over and help Gun Guy lower the cut portion of the tree. It shouldn't take more than ten minutes, assured Log Guy.

While waiting across the street, Gun Guy gave the rope a few tugs, to get a feel for the weight of what was coming. Then, he had a brilliant idea: he tied the rope securely around his waist, to give his body more control and to serve as an anchor, so to speak. Perhaps the wind shifted, the storyteller didn't know for sure. What happened next was unexpected. Gun Guy hunkered down to plant his weight. The tree pulled, he pulled back, the tree kept pulling, he kept pulling back.

Then suddenly, as if in a horse race and the gate had opened, Gun Guy shot across the street, a human battering ram storming the castle, his upper body leaning far ahead of his legs, which were still fighting back in a losing effort to regain control. His body slammed against the fence, several times—SLAP, SLAP, SLAP—as the cut tree tried to defy physics and pull Gun Guy's body through the slats and into the backyard.

A couple of years later and months before acquiring Bandit, one night after eight, someone knocked at our front door. I opened the door and found myself starring, uncomfortably, at Gun Guy. He was wearing an overcoat. What was in his coat pocket, I wondered? This can't be good. Then, he broke the silence and told me he was leaving for vacation in the morning and asked if I'd be willing to keep an eye on his house. I looked him up and down carefully before answering. He was wearing plaid pajama bottoms and bunny slippers and was no longer scary. For that one moment, I saw him as he saw himself: a working man happy to be going on a much-needed vacation. I remembered how Gun Guy had helped Log Guy earlier. I smiled and told him I'd be glad to look after his house.

After all, what are neighbors for?

It Takes a Dog Park to Raise a Deck

Off-the-leash dog parks are a relatively new phenomenon. The world's first official dog park, according to an internet search, opened in 1979 in Berkeley, California, as Ohlone Dog Park. Today, dog parks are the fastest-growing area in the parks and recreation business, with more than 1,200 dog parks currently operating in the U.S. For instance, our hometown for three decades, Portland, Oregon, could claim bragging rights as having the greatest number of dog parks for every 100,000 residents at 5.7, according to a recent study.

Dog parks are not just where dogs go to socialize and meet for play dates. It's also where dog owners meet and form friendships. Unlike our dogs, we may not do any serious butt sniffing, but we willingly engage in cordial conversation, recommend veterinarians, share dog stories, and sometimes see each other later, even away from the park.

Although San Miguel offers many delights and amenities, it lacks a designated dog park open to the public within the city core. To be sure, San Miguel has plenty of attractive parks where you may walk your leashed dog, as well as much open space in the countryside, where you can let your

dog run and hope it eventually returns. But if you want to watch your happy dog romping through a field of grass in a fenced park with other dogs to the tune of "Born Free," well, it's not going to happen in San Miguel. In fact, the second time we lived there, our dog, Duke, had nowhere convenient to relieve himself, let alone run amuck with his homies. We had no lawn, either front or back, and were surrounded by concrete and cobblestones. Every morning and every evening, we'd walk Duke to the small commercial plaza at the end of our street and he would eliminate on a tiny strip of grass adjacent to the plaza parking lot. Eventually, the property owners kept expanding their parking lot, which meant Duke was faced with an ever-decreasing amount of grass, like those unfortunate, heart-wrenching polar bears hovering on melting blocks of ice.

When we decided to move back to Oregon, we wanted to find a house that was reasonably close to a dog park. After five years of Duke trying to hit his spot on a narrow patch of grass like a laser shooting a beam through the eye of a needle, we felt he deserved better. We moved to Medford, a town Arlene and I only knew by passing through it on Interstate-5, traveling either north or south, and occasionally stopping for gas. When we arrived at our new house, we didn't know anybody in that mid-sized town of 85,000 or anything about its neighborhoods, including dog parks.

I suspect, in hindsight, we could not have found a more fulfilling dog park in the entire country than the one we ended up going to every morning in Medford, which was less than three miles from our house. Before long, we were official members of what we came to refer to as "The Dog Parkers." Membership was especially easy for us because of Duke, a big, lovable, adorable Standard Poodle who was a huge people magnet. He greeted strangers with a big smile and was always happy, and, much like Raymond of TV fame, everybody loved Duke. I like to think if they named a bento box dish after Duke, it would be called Miso Happy.

Every morning—rain, shine, snow, or gusty winds—we'd bring Duke to the park, beginning at 9 A.M. for a one-hour visit. It was clearly the highlight of his day and one of our favorite commitments, as well. We went out to lunch or dinner with The Dog Parkers as a group, had pot luck dinners and barbeques at each other's house, visited some amazing wineries together, marched next to each other in political rallies, and each year held a raucous white elephant party during the winter holidays. We shared dog sitting chores and, above all, shared our love of dogs. The dog park featured a Whitman's sampler of the canine family, from Chihuahuas to Great Danes, and just about every breed in-between. One very strange dog, whose name and breed escapes me, used to climb trees.

It was at one Dog Parkers' gathering at our house when the group volunteered to help us rebuild our deck. We knew our deck needed work, but we were content to replace several boards, knock in a few nails, slap stain on the new boards, and clock out for the day. However, one of The Dog Parkers, Hans, an engineer from the Netherlands, shook his head and

said that replacing a few boards wouldn't be good enough. In his precise engineer's diction and well-chosen Dutch words, he told us, "This deck is toast."

And so began our six-week saga of building a deck. As a former condo dweller, I had very little in the way of handyman tools. In fact, my tool chest looked like it was made by Fisher-Price. Granted, I had screw drivers, from regular to Phillips head (Did you ever wonder what this Phillips guy must have looked like, at least from the neck up?), and I had the obligatory one hammer; not to be confused with Thor's Hammer, my hammer could barely pound sand. Don't get me wrong, I had tools. My tool chest, in fact, was well-supplied with masking tape and duct tape, Gorilla Glue and WD-40, a loose collection of nails of all shapes and sizes and enough bolts and screws to tighten Frankenstein's head. I even had a pair of needle-nosed pliers, but only God knows why.

Put another way, if Bob Vila were the vaccine for whatever ails your house, I would be the placebo. That's not to say I was totally without homeowner skills. I worked as a housepainter during college one summer and learned to paint interiors. Hint, it's all about the prep work, which probably explains why I always kept so much masking tape nearby.

Fortunately for us, the rest of The Dog Parkers were better prepared for homeowner duty. Arlene, a former project planner for a computer high-tech company, and Hans worked closely together to develop our attack. After much planning and ordering of materials, we were ready to start

Day 1, the tear-down and removal of our crumbling deck. When our friends arrived that Saturday morning, it was as if I was looking at the cover of a comic book, but the Justice League of America of my pre-teen years had been replaced by my newest team of superheroes: The Dog Parkers. They showed up dressed in work clothes and wearing handyman belts with tools, arriving in pickup trucks, not only ready to tear down the deck but help remove its parts to the wood recycling center. By noon, the old deck was gone.

Soon, we entered a new world with a new vocabulary. We learned about the pros and cons of using composite alternatives, such as Trex®, or the benefits of using pressure-treated wood. Saws of all shapes, sizes, and names were essential, as we found out. We bought a tool that enabled us to easily screw boards together with hidden fasteners from a standing position. We even discovered something known as a palm nailer, a small air-driven tool that made the art of pounding in nails with a hammer obsolete. Hosannas in the highest. If you've already built a deck, these tools are most likely all too familiar and might trigger bad memories. To us, it was all a foreign language and experience. Whereas, Hans named his tools: "Hand me Rudolph."

Most decks sit on concrete pillars. Our previous deck, as an example, sat on wimpy concrete pillars that provided only a modicum of support. Our new deck was going to be different. We dug a dozen holes, two-feet deep and sixteen-inches in diameter. Not by hand, of course. We rented a two-man auger. After working the two-man auger for a spell, I

thought about those hardy men who worked a jack-hammer all-day long to break up concrete in a city. What's life like for them, I wondered? Do they still shake two hours after their shift ends? Can they hold a cup of coffee without spilling? Can they complete a sentence during a conversation without stuttering? I don't know the answers, but I tip my hard hat to them.

Once we had our holes, it was time to fill them with concrete to form industrial-strength pillars. On concrete pour day, The Dog Parkers showed up with their wheel barrows. A concrete-mixing truck poured the wet cement into their wheel barrows, and the race was on. In an hour, all holes were filled and the fasteners were in place. When finished, the deck would be more secure than our house; in case of earthquake, we'll be hunkering under the deck, because our deck was not going anywhere. When it came time to sell, we thought we would advertise our offer as selling a deck with a house attached. The deck was not just solid but gorgeous, thanks to privacy screens and classy black aluminum balusters, all hand-picked by Arlene.

With the construction of the deck behind us, we had one more task to complete. It was time to stain the deck. How hard could that be? A couple of cans of stain, a couple of long-handled brushes, and thou. Plus, I had house painting experience. Right?

Harder than we thought, as it turned out. We're not sure where we went wrong. Perhaps we selected the wrong stain, a color that looked more like an orange ice cream bar than a cedar plank, or applied the stain too late in the day and too unevenly, or didn't prep the deck properly. There were four of us working in the hot July sun to stain the deck. All for naught, as it turned out.

In reading about screenplays, I came across a piece of storytelling advice. It said at the point in the story where everything seems hunky-dory, it is so not. There was neither hunky nor dory waiting for us at the end of that day. The deck staining was, as they say, an unmitigated disaster. Its color was dreadful, its streaks everywhere. We let wishful thinking get the better of our thoughts and told ourselves it would look better in the morning. We might as well have been sitting in a life boat in the middle of the Atlantic watching *The Titanic* sink and foolishly thinking maybe the ship will float back to the top by breakfast. Our newly stained deck didn't improve over-night. If anything, it looked worse: uneven splotches of orange covered the deck like the heartbreak of psoriasis.

A tom-tom beat rippled through our community and before long all of The Dog Parkers knew what had happened. A few called to try and ease our grief. Even Hans, the chief architect and driving force behind the building of our deck, a man who was at our house every morning by eight and stayed until two in the afternoon, for the better part of six weeks, I might add, called to remind us that it was only a deck and to not worry about the staining job.

But, to us, it was more than just a deck. A few days later, we hired a professional deck staining company and they

corrected our mistake, covering the deck with a stain that was closer to cedar than bright orange.

We christened it Duke's Deck and rightly so, for without our wonderful dog, we would have never known about The Dog Parkers in the first place or formed such rewarding friendships. A dog is a homeowner's best friend.

Good Cats, Bad Cats

Let's face it, cats don't have to play jazz to be cool. If a cat walks into a room, he does so radiating self-assurance. It's as if a Royal Court Trumpeter has announced the arrival of a distinguished ambassador at the Court of St. James. The carpet has been rolled out and everyone in the room is awe-struck or should be: women fan themselves and swoon, men automatically cover their codpiece with their hands, dogs run for cover.

Now if that same strolling cat were to see something move out of the corner of his eye, he would immediately freeze for the smallest of moments and slowly turn his head in the direction of the moving object. At that point, the cat would suddenly turn philosophical and have one existential thought. Is that something I can eat or is that something that can eat me?

A cat is one of the most lethal predators in the world, pound for pound perhaps the deadliest. But I'm getting ahead of myself. When we bought our first house in Portland, after many years of apartment living, one of our initial home improvements was to get a cat, which we set out to do

before we had even finished unpacking. We looked through something known as the Nickel Want Ads, a listing of opportunities within the local community printed on yellow paper. It connected those looking to acquire something with those looking to get rid of something. We found what we wanted under a "free to good home" category for unwanted pets. We called ahead and made an appointment to pick up a cat. However, once we got there, the owner "up-sold" us on taking two cats, not just one, using the old canard that they'll play together and be happier. I suspect he sold used cars during the week and did rather well at it. Still, we agreed. After spending thirty minutes watching the man chase down two semi-domesticated cats from his backyard and secure them in individual pet carriers, we were on our way. Once home with our latest home improvements, we immediately showed both cats where to find their litter box, in a small room that was once part of the garage. Then, we put down water and food for the cats and went about taking care of other chores. The cats, I should mention, were ravenous and ate as if they had been stranded on a small island with an inedible volley ball named Wilson.

I remember, it was a warm September day and we kept the front door slightly open to get air moving through the house. We continued unpacking and putting things away. Arlene worked the downstairs area, while I was handling upstairs. Not long into our tasks, Arlene came upstairs and asked me if I had seen the cats. I said no. We searched the house for the cats, calling out by their given-names—we hadn't had them long enough to even pick new names, one of the key benefits of owning an animal that has no meaningful control over his or her life. We checked outside, walking up and down the street, combing through our double-lot-sized backyard with mature growth. No cats.

Arlene was distraught. Not even half-a-day in as a new mother and she had already lost her brood. It seemed the cats had fled the scene. What to do? After several minutes of grieving, we shrugged our shoulders and decided to try it again. Stiff upper lip and all that; time to move on. We looked at the Nickel Want Ads one more time and found a different ad for free cats to good homes. This time the person was a specialist in finding homes for cats and lived nearby. She was, in a word, a Cat Lady.

The Cat Lady interviewed us for twenty minutes, smiled and said she could tell we'd be good cat guardians. We didn't have the heart or courage to tell her we just lost our first two cats less than an hour ago but selfishly thought we should give cat ownership another try. Her place was full of cats, a scene out of a Mother Goose rhyme. On the kitchen counter, she had a terrified hamster running in a wheel. Watching below were cats waiting for their chance to pounce. In her backyard, a mob of cats stood under a tall bird feeder, like vultures hanging around Deadman's Curve anticipating roadkill.

She gave us her rock star cats of the moment, a brother and sister pair named Antony and Cleopatra, respectively. Antony (Tony) was a mostly black Tuxedo cat, with a

single black spot on his white furry face. Cleopatra (Cleo) was also bi-color but predominately white with a touch of black. Together, they were gorgeous, and we were excited to bring home both. However, the Cat Lady was not quite done. She gave us a stack of cat magazines, as well as food, toys, and two pet carriers. And all of this was for free. Walking away from her house, carrying our new cats, we felt as proud as if we had just passed the state bar exam in the upper five percentile.

As soon as we opened the pet carriers and introduced Tony and Cleo to their new home, our first two cats reappeared. Uh-oh. It turned out, the two cats, their hunger satisfied with full bellies, fell asleep on our dining room chairs, and their presence was hidden by the dining room table cloth. But now, with competition entering their territory, the two cats were wide awake and ready to defend their turf. Clearly, we were over-achievers. We had started the day thinking of getting only one cat and now we had four. Unfortunately, the four did not get along, with every cat hissing and spitting, and not one of them using the litter box. It was a tough night.

The next morning, we decided we had to take one set of cats back to their original owner. Now, there was no way we were going back to the Cat Lady and returning her two cats. We did everything but donate a kidney to get those cats. Honor has its limits; last in, first out was not going to cut it. So, Arlene called the first cat-owner and said her husband, that would be me, was allergic to the cats and was having a difficult time breathing—and that would be true. I'm allergic to cats, or, more precisely, animal dander, and I'm asthmatic. We drove the first two cats back and left them with their previous owner, despite his protestations. I like to think of it as the reverse of a repo.

Eventually, Tony and Cleo settled nicely into their new home. We even installed a cat door, leading to the backyard. But two months later, Cleo had a heart attack after getting spayed, a rare post-surgical complication, and died. When we didn't return home from the veterinarian with Cleo, Tony spent hours in the backyard meowing in a dreadful, deep-throated moan, as if keening over the loss of his sister. It was heart-breaking. So, we decided to get another cat. Instead of turning to the Nickel Want Ads, we visited a pet store, where we purchased a young calico. We named her Elly, short for T.S. Eliot.

Elly was a shorthaired calico, which, as I learned later, is not a breed but a description of its tri-color combination. She was mostly white and orange, with a few black spots as accent colors. Because she was a calico, she was the most generic of all domestic house cats. She was affectionate, chatty, and opinionated. When we returned home from work, she would follow us around the house, voicing her opinions at our heels. I imagined she was complaining about us not leaving enough water or not cleaning the litter box often enough or forgetting to leave the TV on. Calico cats are referred to as "money cats," because they are supposed to bring good fortune. Although we can't say with certainty that Elly was a money cat, she did bring us much love over the years and for that we were very fortunate. Even Tony accepted her immediately. He groomed her for days, probably trying to get rid of the pet shop smell.

Elly was the curious cat; Tony the hunter. Before long, we fully understood the disadvantage of a cat door. Our backyard was full of shrubs and trees, and small animals lurked about. Tony would bring surprises for us through the cat door; small mice or small birds, and most often those ill-fated creatures would be dead. I expected one night to see him drag a severed human arm through the cat door. Not all were D.O.A., however. One afternoon, he brought in a wounded but very much still alive mid-sized bird. We don't know how he caught it or carried it through the tiny cat door. But he did. And there we were, chasing a bird in our house. Tony watched, calmly licking his paws, in mild amusement, perhaps thinking my job here is done. Elly joined us in running through the house trying to recapture and release the bird, which we finally did, but only after knocking over furniture, including two book cases and all the books on them. I caught the bird and released it outside. As far as we could tell, the bird was understandably frantic and in shock but it flew away, muttering obscenities under its breath.

One time when we had a friend staying with us Tony showed off his hunting skills. Our friend was in the TV room watching a show, which was a room converted from the garage by the previous owner. A smaller room off of it housed our washer and dryer, the litter box, and the infamous cat door. Arlene was in bed resting. I was at the dining room table drawing. That's when I heard our friend ask several questions in rapid fire: "What is that?" What'd you do?" "Is that thing alive?" Tony, it seems, had caught a mouse, brought it through the cat door, and placed it at our friend's feet, waiting for the adulation he was due. Nice kitty. Instead? Apparently, one cat's gift is another person's freak-out. She screamed and ran by me as if trying to catch a bus, and joined Arlene in the other room, closing the door behind her.

Lesson learned. We decided it was safer to invest in litter boxes than in cat doors, so from that point on our cats became true housecats. No more trips to the outside world for our feline friends, and we settled in to become their obedient servants.

Scratchy

Even with their legendary nine lives, cats still don't live long enough. Then, there is the occasional exception, such as our last cat who unfortunately seemed to live forever.

In the case of our previous cats, Tony and Elly, we didn't want to see them cross over the Rainbow Bridge. Losing them left a big hole in our lives. Our relationship with their successor, Sadie, was a different story along the lines of "Here's your hat, what's your hurry?" She was never easy to live with. She rarely curled up with you, and when she did you waited for her insanity to kick in and you were suddenly and viciously attacked, emerging as if you had gone through a paper shredder. Sadie didn't rub-up against you affectionately. She didn't purr. When she meowed, which wasn't often, it was usually a curt and loud guttural meow coming from the deepest pit of her body, as if you had reached Satan's answering machine and were told to leave a message. We all lived in fear of triggering one of Sadie's moods or unexpectedly crossing her path. If we were to erect a statue of Sadie in a public park, it would show her not sitting on a horse or eating from a food bowl, but standing on a sofa with her eyes squinting and right front paw raised, poised to pounce and strike a lethal blow. She never weighed more than seven pounds.

Sadie was a rescue cat who never fully appreciated being rescued. When our friend and neighbor, Mary, picked Sadie, as I imagine out of a lineup, from the local animal shelter and brought her home, it wasn't long before she realized Sadie did not work well or play well with others. Since Mary had two older cats and the arrival of Sadie terrified them both, the newest member was going to have to go. Mary offered us Sadie and we accepted. Now if I had a time machine and could go back to 1982, I'd buy Apple stock, which at time sold for as low as twenty-three cents a share. A time machine could improve my life in so many ways. I'd use it, for instance, to go back in time and turn down Mary's generous offer of a free kitten who already had all of her shots.

In defense of Sadie, she was gorgeous, a part-Siamese mix with striking blue eyes. She kept to herself. She didn't require expensive cat food that resembled pâté at a French restaurant; she only ate the cheap crunchy stuff. She used her litter box, at least until late in life. She rarely went outside, and when she did, she stayed close to home. Of course, she scratched furniture, but she was monogamous about it and usually kept to the same chair. Best of all, she always seemed healthy. She never required more than the very minimum of costly visits to the vet. Still, she was often a royal pain in the ass.

Take the time one of our neighbors stopped by for a drink and a chat. We lived in a 10-story condo building in downtown Portland, in an area known as King's Hill. Our living room and dining room offered commanding views of the surrounding landscape. We could see three volcanoes, one of the most important rivers in American history (the Columbia River), and the thriving cityscape below. To ensure we made good use of the room, we had banished our television set to the second bedroom. Visiting with friends in our living room became a much-appreciated diversion in our lives. On this particular late afternoon, we shared wine and small bites with a man who lived on our floor. He was friendly, intelligent, a good conversationist. He was always nicely groomed and well dressed, to the point of being fastidious. At one point during a harmless bit of chatter, something spooked Sadie and she ran up the man's face with her sharp claws out, like a rock climber scaling El Capitan. In a manner of seconds, our friend's nice shirt was drenched in wine and his clean face was covered in tiny scratches, all of which were bleeding. As he left our unit, he told us the next time he saw that cat, he would be carrying a blow torch.

It was a common reaction to her. Those most familiar with Sadie's attitude coined new names for the cat: Satan, Sadistic Sadie, Devil Cat, Scratchy, along with names that should not appear in this book on advice of the cat's attorney. And Sadie's bites were far worse than her scratches, forcing us to keep a container of bandages and a tube of Neosporin nearby at all times. We concluded she was psychotic. If there were a nationwide network of mental health clinics for troubled cats, a Betty Ford Clinic for Felines, we would have had her committed a long time ago.

Again, don't get me wrong, Sadie had her charms. She was pleasing to look at and petite enough to never appear threatening. If we had guests, she would always walk in to see who was there. Well-meaning strangers would instantly pick her up, leaving us little time to warn them. They'd hold her and rub her belly and say sweet "nice kitty" things until, within minutes, they'd be nursing a new wound and Sadie would be running away to hide under a bed. Regular visitors stayed away from Sadie; scratch me once, as they say.

Several months after the loss of our first Standard Poodle, Cassie, we were asked by friends to take care of their Standard Poodle, Rio, for a weekend. We agreed. Rio was still a puppy but weighed close to fifty pounds. Arlene and I were downstairs in the kitchen, when we heard a noise upstairs that sounded like a cattle stampede. It was Rio, followed closely by Sadie. She cornered the terrified dog in the kitchen and raised a paw, ready to strike. Rio's eyes were wide with fear. We told Sadie to put the paw down and step away. She did and we continued as before; unfortunately, young Rio had been scarred for life.

One of the best compliments I can give Sadie is that she traveled well. She was with us the first time we spent six days in a car driving from Portland to San Miguel. She made the first return trip to the States with us, too. She rode stoically in her crate for our second six-day road trip to San Miguel and back-again several years later. Other than spending an extra twenty minutes every morning trying to catch her to put her in the crate, she wasn't a bother. She was a sun-worshipper and found the climate in Mexico much more to her liking than those rainy days in the Willamette Valley.

The concept of "aging out of crime" contends that as a person ages the individual is less likely to commit another crime. It was a foreign concept to Sadie. She seemed to get meaner as she got older, that is, until one morning she had a seizure. The vet ran tests and did Sadie's blood work but found nothing significant to report. The vet suggested we try an MRI. When we were told how much an MRI for an old cat would cost, we passed on the idea. The vet said we might be lucky and it could have been a rare seizure, a one-off, so to speak. We were told to watch her carefully and bring her back in if she had another fit.

Sadie didn't have another seizure but was surprisingly much calmer after her one and only fit. This led us to believe for many years she, indeed, had been possessed by Satan, which had soured her views on life and people, in general, and forced her to leave her radar dial on attack mode. It wasn't her fault. To borrow from the words of comedian Flip Wilson, "The devil made her do it."

We've come to believe the seizure was her body performing a long overdue exorcism. And we believe it worked, for her final six months were peaceful. The six months after that and beyond have been even more peaceful for us. Better late than never.

Ask Dr. Expat

If you do a Google search for tips on moving to Mexico, you'll find many useful articles, everything from the differences in visa types to why you need to visit your local consulate before moving here. You can learn more about the legal and financial requirements for picking up stakes and heading south or find a transportation company willing to negotiate your personal items across an international border without having to fork off an enormous bribe.

But if you really want to learn the unvarnished truth about life in San Miguel, you'll need to study at the feet of Dr. Expat ("I'm not a real doctor but I play one on Zoom").

Dear Dr. Expat,

I'm planning a move to San Miguel and am wondering about the weather. I know I could just check the Web, but anybody can post anything these days. That's why, I prefer to hear first-hand from a local authority on what to expect, weather-wise and snow-wise, especially from a doctor. Please advise. Thanks.

Wisconsin Cheesehead

Dear Cheesehead,

Unfortunately, I'm afraid I have mostly bad news to share. I hate to break it to you, but we don't get a lot of snow in San Miguel. In fact, we don't get any, with the possible exception of an occasional brief dusting in the mountains that resembles powdered sugar on a donut and disappears about as fast as you can eat a donut. This means you will not need your snow shovel, fancy snow blower, or even fancier snow plow. Leave your snow shoes, skis, and hockey stick behind, as well. And don't even think about bringing your own Zamboni with you. There is still good news for you, I think. You can keep your bulky winter sweaters and heavy jackets with a gazillion pockets. You're going to need to wear such winter garb inside your house. Although here in winter it might be 75-degrees outside, inside you'll feel like a two-legged popsicle stick.

Dear Dr. Expat,

I've heard that you may not need a car living in San Miguel. However, I can't envision living without one. In fact, I love everything about cars, become very attached to my cars, and have a habit of naming them. What do I need to do to prepare Sylvia for living in the middle of Mexico?

Tommy

Dear Tommy,

I'm assuming Sylvia is a car and will not need to learn Spanish. That said, I always recommend drivers practice three habits before moving here. The first is to learn how to drive in reverse gear and down the wrong way of a one-way street. It may take you several attempts—and a few traffic tickets—to get accustomed to going backward instead of forward, but to live in San Miguel you should be skilled enough to drive in reverse, for at least a quarter of a mile at a time. The second is to make sure your car has several dings and scratches, as well as a broken side mirror, already on it before bringing the car here. This will make it easier on you, say, after you've been here a month and your precious car starts looking like you bought it at a Demolition Derby fire sale. The streets are narrow, cars are parked haphazardly, and, well, accidents happen. And the third is to remove all your hubcaps. Driving with hubcaps is considered a sign of cultural arrogance and should be avoided at all costs. After all, you do want to fit in. As a follow-up, I recommend you install high-grade shock absorbers. Trust me, you'll be glad you did. In Mexico, speed bumps are known as *topes*, and in my experience, calling a *tope* a speed bump is like calling a skyscraper a mobile home. That pretty much takes care of your car question, Tommy. Now, what about you? I encourage you to rethink your habit of assigning cars names. To cure you of this habit, try watching the old TV series *My Mother the Car.* Attributing human traits to a motorized vehicle could be a sign of mental decline, as it was for the creators of that show.

Dear Dr. Expat,

My wife and I are conflicted about moving to San Miguel. Although we pay an arm and a leg—not literally,

yet—for what we consider sub-standard medical care in the U.S., we're afraid to live without it. Is it still worth taking the plunge? What we need to know before relocating is what kind of healthcare can we expect to find in San Miguel?

Frank & April

Dear Frank and April,

The keyword in understanding medical care in this town is patience. If you send your physician an email requesting an appointment, it could take from an hour to the next day to get your appointment. And when you do, you'll need to set aside at least thirty minutes for your doctor to examine you, sometimes even longer. The visit might cost as much as $30 USD or about the same as a co-pay in the U.S.

In addition, the town has more small pharmacies than Seattle has small coffee shops; filling a prescription often costs about the same as ordering a Guatemala Antigua Venti at Starbucks. It also has inexpensive yet reliable labs. For example, my wife needed to confirm her blood type before getting a Mexican driver's license. Oddly enough, this minor, potentially life-saving data point is not on your American driver's license. Hmm.

Anyway, she stopped in a public lab, waited in line for a few minutes, had a small amount of blood drawn, waited another five minutes, and walked out with an official print out of her blood type. The cost? Three $USD, as in three dollars. The only way she could have verified her blood type for less in the States is if she had it done at the Dollar

Store. If you're into alternative medical treatments, you'll have many options, from energy and sound healers to a more traditional *curandera* or *bruja*. The latter will especially come in handy in case you want to cast a spell on a former in-law or boss.

Dear Dr. Expat,
What's up with all the violence in Mexico?
Nervous Nellie

Dear Nervous Nellie,

What's up with all the violence in America? I don't think I need to point out that violence is a world-wide problem and certainly not limited to Mexico. But I do want to point out that citizens in this country are not allowed to openly carry firearms, unlike in more primitive parts of the world such as Texas and Missouri. Yes, violence remains a part of the Mexican culture. A key distinction is that in Mexico, violence is more personal and domestic and not wildly random. It is generally considered safe for kids to go to school or for anyone to visit a movie theater or mall. You never hear of a mass shooting in a grocery store in Mexico committed by a guy who just bought an assault rifle days or weeks earlier. My point is, you are probably safer here than just about anywhere north of Mexico or south of Canada, with a relatively lawless land existing between those two borders.

I should also mention that street crime does occur in San Miguel, which is why my preferred solution is to keep

two wallets. My real wallet is in my house, so cleverly hidden that only an astute video gamer might find it. On the other hand, my fake wallet—the one I carry with me at all times—is filled with expired credit cards from stores that no longer exist, an old tattered library card from the 90s, photos of strangers, images that came with the wallet, and a few worthless business cards I've collected over the years. I also throw in a legitimate 20-peso note and an unused condom, because I don't want to humiliate the thief. Give him at least a little something for his effort worth bragging about is my motto. As an aside, I heard about an expat who put itching powder in his fake wallet, expecting any person who took his wallet to find himself eventually covered in the powder. Unfortunately, one time when the expat was sitting on the wallet the itching powder packet opened. That was three years ago, and he's still constantly scratching his behind. My advice is to not let the cure be worse than the disease, whatever you decide.

Dear Dr. Expat,

I recently listened to a podcast that said I should plan to wear liared clothing in San Miguel. What is liared clothing, where might I find it, and why would it be necessary? Confused

Dear Confused,

Your signature says it all. It's not "liared" clothing but "layered" clothing. The air temperature in this town can vary by twenty-degrees at the same point in time, depending upon which side of the street you're on. If you're walking on the shady side, for instance, you'll need a sweater, but cross to the sunny side of the street and suddenly you're shvitzing. I suggest you see a local audiologist at your earliest convenience.

Dear Dr. Expat,

When I mentioned I was thinking about moving to San Miguel, someone told me it was the City of Fallen Women. I find the notion titillating. However, I could not find anything online about a "red-light" district there, something like what they have in Amsterdam, if you know what I'm saying. Could you recommend a map or guidebook that could direct me to the real action? Asking for a friend.

Randy

Dear Randy,

I'm assuming Randy is your real name and not a description of your libido—or maybe it's both. Either way, you clearly lack critical thinking and reading comprehension skills, my friend. Let me set you straight. The phrase "fallen women" when referring to life in San Miguel does not mean women who have fallen from grace. It is describing women who have fallen less gracefully on one of our treacherous public streets.

Unlike where you might currently live, our streets are paved with coarse stones and uneven stretches of concrete, sport unexpected gaps or steel protrusions, all made more

dangerous by the constant splashing of soapy water by store vendors. When you walk here, you need to do so as gingerly as if you're walking through a Colombian minefield. Let me put it another way, can you chew gum and dance at the same time? Well, that's what walking in San Miguel is like. If you spend too much time admiring the blue sky while walking, you are destined to fall flat on your face. In your case, that would make you, ahem, a Fallen Man.

Dear Dr. Expat,

I have a highly sensitive stomach. Just reading a description of the Pepperoni Jalapeno Pizza from Little Caesar's makes me queasy. On the other hand, my husband has the reverse problem and can eat anything in large portions, no matter how spicy. Which means I often find myself waiting for him to get out of the bathroom. We're looking at retiring to San Miguel and wanted to know how best to prepare our respective stomach problems for life south of the border. Comments?

Distressed Stomach

Dear Distressed Stomach,

What you describe is a common fear about eating in another country. When Americans visit Mexico, for example, they can sometimes fall victim to what's known as "Montezuma's Revenge." When Mexicans visit America, they often suffer a similar fate in what's known as "The Empire Strikes Back." My point is, you're not alone. We all have stomachs.

Interesting fact: despite what you might have heard (no pun intended), cows only have one stomach. But, and here's the catch, each cow stomach has four departments. So, if you were a cow, you wouldn't have this problem. You could just assign one of your stomach departments the responsibility for handling spicy food, leaving the other three departments for normal digestion. Since you're not a cow, however, here's what I propose: rent or buy a place with at least two bathrooms, perhaps as many as four. It will save your marriage.

Which brings me to another critical data point, input begets output and plumbing can be tricky down here. This city is very old and its plumbing is even older. There's a good chance you will not be able to flush toilet paper down your toilet. Instead, you will be required to place the used paper in a trash can next to the toilet. It's not that hard, once you get used to the process. That said, I encourage you to practice this at home before moving here. Finally, bring plenty of soft tissues with you to avoid getting a case of the red-ass. The toilet paper here can give sandpaper a run for its money. And no matter where you go in this city, you'll always want to carry toilet paper with you, just not on the bottom of your shoe.

Dear Dr. Expat,

I love to travel but my problem is I am a very light sleeper. How light, you ask? If someone sneezes in the middle of the night in Timbuktu, I'm the first one to shout "Gesundheit." I've been told that San Miguel can be noisy. If so, what can I do to help overcome the noise factor and ensure I get enough

sleep while living there?

Sleepy

Dear Sleepy,

Your concerns are valid. This town is literally and figuratively a string of fire crackers attached to a car horn stuck inside a hip-hop concert. And that's not even mentioning the dogs, which are everywhere and are not afraid to bark their opinions—at all hours, non-stop, as is their nature. Or the lonely *borrachos* singing sad love songs in the empty lot next door (I daresay a metaphor for their personal lives). Or the interminable and inexplicable ringing of church bells. The last person to try and make sense of the various chimes in this town was hospitalized. So, unless you wear a hearing aid, your best solution will be to jam cotton balls into your ears at night or invest in noise-cancelling ear plugs made of silicone.

There is, of course, the flip side of your problem, which is not hearing when you need to hear. Yes, our town is noisy but some of the noise is meant for the quick communication of much-needed services. For instance, the men who pick up your garbage clang a bell loudly just before arriving. People who ride around on bikes and sharpen knives also have a distinct sound announcing their arrival. This is true for traveling food carts and gas deliveries, as well. So, it's not as if you can or should turn off your sense of hearing all the time. If all else fails, before retiring at night try a hardy dose of CBD oil and two shots of tequila. I hope that answers your question, Sleepy. Best regards to Wheezy and Grouchy.

Dear Dr. Expat,

I'm a proud member of a dying breed. I don't care if I offend someone's feelings, and I don't go for any of that politically correct nonsense spouted by snowflakes. I'm a cantankerous old curmudgeon living in the backwoods of Vermont who last smiled in 1986, when Billy Buckner cost the Boston Red Sox the World Series. What advice do you have for me in fitting in San Miguel?

Proud Codger

Dear Proud Codger,

My simple advice to you is if you want to move to San Miguel, you must drop the codger nonsense and learn to smile. The people in this town are extremely courteous and greet even strangers on the street with a "Buenos días" or "Good Morning" and ask how they are doing, which is obviously a foreign concept to you. True, you might find another grumpy old man or two down here to suit your fancy, enough perhaps for a game of three-handed pinochle. I suggest you avoid the sunlight and only go out at night, stay away from garlic, and watch out for wooden crosses. This town is full of them, crosses and garlic, that is.

As a life-long sports gambler, I should mention I also smiled when Buckner made that error. I had a substantial bet down on the Mets to win the series. Sometimes life is good. Apparently, in your case, life is never good. So, on second thought, stay north in your Unabomber cabin. We don't need your kind in San Miguel.

Still Spanglish After All These Years

My friend Larry, a long-time expat resident of San Miguel, has a theory about personal safety. According to Larry, if you see a tough-looking adult Mexican male on the street walking toward you and you're not sure if he's dangerous, relax. All you need do is make eye-contact, smile, and say, "Buenos días." Larry is convinced that the man would smile back and warmly reply, "Buenos días" and go on his way. That's because, according to Larry's theory, there isn't a man in the entire country that would accost you after such a greeting. The people in this gracious country are raised to be polite, to return a courtesy with a courtesy.

Which pleases me because I'm still unable to master Spanish, other than deliver clipped greetings, pose simple questions, and tell people my name—all in present tense, like a three-year-old. This is a sad and unfortunate admission. I was taught Spanish by Latin American nuns in the lower grades and have the report card to prove it. I took one year of high school Spanish. And I spent nine months while serving in the United States military on the island of Puerto Rico. Still, *no comprendo mucho.*

If I had mastered Spanish, I wouldn't have to settle for a mere "Good morning." When greeted by a stranger in town, I could launch a more detailed response.

Me: Buenos días.

Stranger: Buenos días.

Me: [In Spanish, because in this fantasy I'm fluent) Do you have a minute? I wanted to ask you about walking in this town and it's not just the holes in the pavement and those large steel extensions that stick out from the ground unexpectedly to trip you or the dog stuff that's everywhere. My question is mostly about the cobblestones. Do you wear special shoes? I must be doing something wrong because every time I go for a walk I feel like I'm getting my spine readjusted. Not only that, but these cobblestones are killing the base of my feet. I don't think it's anything serious like deep vein thrombosis. Who needs a clot, am I right? But, here's the deal. Sometimes I walk and I can't feel anything in my feet. Other times, it hurts like hell. Still other times, I feel a tingling sensation. So, I'm thinking maybe it's just old-fashioned bursitis, especially since I'm doing more walking these days and I'm getting older. Of course, I was immediately worried about having diabetes, both level one and level two diabetes run in my family. Not sure I know the difference between the two levels, anyway. Do you? My point is I read someplace where diabetes can cause foot pain. But I don't seem to have other signs of being diabetic and my last blood panel workup came back fine. So, I'm thinking maybe it's not diabetes. Maybe it's gout, because of all the

wine I've been drinking and wine creates uric acid, which is one of the causes of gout. This Happy Hour business every day in San Miguel is ruining my health. Really. You know what I mean? I'm probably drinking too much Oso Negro Gin. Do you prefer gin or vodka for a martini? Sorry. That was out of line. You probably don't like martinis at all and prefer tequila. But it can't be gout. I recall that's mostly a big toe thing and my big toes are working fine, so I ruled out gout. Now I'm thinking the pain is a sign of plantar fasciitis, because it's mostly in my heel. Do you know the best shoes to wear if you think you have plantar fasciitis?

The Stranger would sprint down the street, casting concerned glances my way to ensure he was not being followed.

Me: Wait. Don't leave. I'm haven't told you about my stomach disorder yet. I think I might have a parasite. What should I take for it?

In retrospect, it's a good thing I am not proficient at Spanish. Such one-sided conversations could set back cordial American and Mexican diplomatic relations several decades.

It's not as if I didn't try to learn Spanish. I did. I came. I studied. But I didn't conquer. English is the common language of the modern world, which is a huge comfort for me, since I was fortunate to have been born in America and, after six decades of trying, it is obvious that English remains the only language I will ever fully know. It's a good thing I wasn't born in Finland, because I'd never be able to speak Finnish.

I attended a book reading by an author who wrote of his long-time experiences living in Mexico, especially his years in San Miguel. During the Q&A period that followed, one woman said she thought the biggest problem in San Miguel today was English-speaking expats who don't take the time to study and become fluent in Spanish.

Mexico is a gorgeous country, full of wonderful people, enormous resources, and great promise. But I believe it has bigger problems than Americans not fluently conversing with their neighbors in Spanish. There's the poverty rate, the huge gap between the haves and have nots, the lack of economic opportunity, insufficient education, systemic graft and corruption, and, of course, the very serious matter of drug cartels and violence. One's inability to exchange pleasantries in Spanish pales by comparison.

San Miguel de Allende, like it or not, for good or bad, is a sophisticated international destination, where it helps to know Spanish but it is hardly the main requirement for residency. Would my life here be enhanced if I were proficient in the local jargon? Yes, no question about it. Is my experience of living here diminished by mostly speaking English and only occasionally taking a stab a Spanish? Rarely.

Instead of taking a class in conversational Spanish, I suppose if I really wanted to break down the language barrier, I would volunteer to teach English as a second language. Because this is a bi-lingual town, a Mexican worker who speaks

both Spanish and English has a better chance of finding a job, especially in the service industry, which dominates the local economy. On the other hand, when the aging American who studies Spanish dies, his Spanish expires with him, along with his passport, AARP membership card, and last bottle of lisinopril tablets.

All this is moot, of course, because I'm afraid the only way I will become fluent in Spanish at this point in my life is if I'm found guilty of a crime and sent to a Mexican prison. Necessity, after all, is the mother of language acquisition. In fact, I'm already planning to memorize a few key prison survival phrases in Spanish, just in case my next career stop is a turn in the slammer:

Por última *vez, no quiero bañarme contigo.* (For the last time, I do not want to shower with you.)

Por favor, deja de agitar esa cosa en mi cara. (Please, quit waving that thing in my face.)

And my personal favorite:

Estoy muy viejo para ser tu perra. Voy a tener que ser tu madre. (I'm too old to be your bitch. I'll have to be your mother.)

Mi Casa es Su Casa

In one of many iconic scenes in the British television show "Downton Abbey," The Dowager Countess of Grantham, played by Dame Maggie Smith, sarcastically asked her fellow aristocratic dinner companions, "What is a weekend?" If you're a retired expat living in San Miguel, the answer is simple: every day. That's not to say an expat is lazy and spends his or her time roasting outdoors like sun-kissed apples or shooting grouse with the Crawleys. On the contrary, the typical expat in this town is never bored. A common refrain is to hear someone say they woke up in the morning with nothing to do and by the end of the day only got half of it done.

Expats keep busy in this town—and so we did, especially the second time we lived here. In addition to volunteering and attending book readings, plays, and art gallery openings, we entertained. A lot. We had an ideal house for handling a party. The house, itself, was modest in size, consisting of two large bedrooms with *bóveda* ceilings; two large *en suite* bathrooms, one with a jetted tub featuring jets that looked cool but didn't work; a decent-sized living room area

open on one side to a charming interior courtyard with a fountain; a back courtyard with the obligatory broken glass on the top of walls; and enough off-street parking for 2.5 cars. Nothing fancy and no spectacular views.

Ah, but what about the kitchen? The kitchen, unfortunately, was the smallest room in the house, offering little in the way of counter space, a single sink, a narrow fridge, and a gas stove that would occasionally explode when turning on the pilot light. Three people could stand in the kitchen at the same time, as long as nobody moved. This was the house we rented on Stirling Dickinson.

When we moved into the Stirling Dickinson house, we were told our furniture from the States would arrive in four weeks, guaranteed. It took seven weeks. The transportation company was so embarrassed they knocked fifteen percent off of our final bill, something unheard of down here or anywhere, especially a rebate offered by a company's own volition. The joyous day finally arrived and a large moving van pulled up to our house. After spending seven weeks without furniture and only a smattering of household goods, we were ecstatic. When they started unloading crates, I had them stop and told them they had the wrong house. They set out a few unfamiliar pieces of furniture, pieces that didn't belong to us; our things were indeed in the van, as it turned out, but placed at the wrong end, toward the front and not the back.

The movers asked if I had a hammer, and I told them yes, but it was in my tool chest, which was packed with our things still in the van. Eventually, the movers found a way to reach our belongings, and we started the slow process of putting things away and arranging furniture. We had a home.

Our first Christmas in the house was truly festive. Along with two neighbors, we hosted a progressive Christmas dinner buffet for nearly one-hundred friends. Two doors east of us, our neighbor, Mary, hosted the cocktail hour; two doors west from us, Kate, another neighbor and friend, hosted the dessert course. In-between, Arlene and I provided the main courses, with Arlene doing all of the cooking. I tended bar in the interior courtyard. Before people arrived, we had what we thought was an enormous amount of food; but soon a long line formed outside our door and snaked down the street. Everyone showed up at the same time. Fifteen minutes after they arrived, we had little left to show for it. As one person said to me, "My God, they're eating like vultures." It was a deliciously memorable evening.

All three households were exhausted from the experience, so for next Christmas we did not hold another progressive dinner. Instead, Arlene and I entertained fewer friends with a buffet-style dinner for seventy at our house. The year after, we dropped the number to roughly thirty. Our final Christmas was an intimate dinner for eleven. Had we stayed through one more Christmas, I suspect we would have dined alone.

One Christmas season we hosted a small gathering for a *posada*. The word *posada* means "inn" or "shelter" in Spanish. This tradition re-enacts Mary and Joseph's journey to Bethlehem and their search for a place to stay. This is the "no room at the inn" celebration, something that could have

been avoided had Travelocity been available to the Holy Family. *Posadas* take place over nine nights in neighborhoods all over Mexico, with a different house selected each night. Our neighbor David arranged with the local parish to have the procession stop at our house on one of the nights. We invited guests to join us. Arlene made food to eat, and I made hot buttered rum to drink. A *posada* is a beautiful service to watch. The procession held candles and sang. Half of the procession stayed outside and sang, asking if there was room at the inn. The other half entered our house and sang back, denying them entrance and telling them to hit the bricks. I poured the priest, who didn't speak English but, apparently, was happy to drink in any language, a cup of hot buttered rum. As the procession was ready to continue on its way, a woman serving as the priest's translator approached me and, in English, asked a favor. She handed me a thermos. The priest, she explained, loved the hot buttered rum and asked if you wouldn't mind filling up his container so he could take some with him.

It wasn't just dinner parties. We also hosted a monthly movie night called "Guilty Pleasures Night." The idea started with eight friends and eventually grew to the unmanageable number of thirty-five. On the third Wednesday of every month, we would open our house to movie night. I referred to it as a "guilty pleasure" because the films I selected were not art house flicks or foreign movies or the latest incarnation of *Citizen Kane*, but chosen for their entertainment value solely. Movies were most often comedies from the 70s and

80s (*Midnight Run; My Cousin Vinny; The Freshman; Saint Ralph; Cold Comfort Farm*); as well as enduring classics, including *Some Like it Hot* and *The African Queen*. Nothing too heavy or taxing. The idea was to check your brain at the door, so to speak, and have fun.

Guests would arrive, bearing food and drink, at six P.M. and for the next hour we would all eat, drink, and be Mary or Harry or Larry and Moe. For the next two hours, we'd watch a movie. Before anyone arrived, we would stage our living room to more closely fit a movie theater setting. We pulled our sofa closer to the TV and cleared everything else out of the room to make way for an odd collection of mismatched chairs, whatever we had or needed. The interior courtyard was turned over to a bar. We referred to the sofa as the mosh pit because Duke would sprawl out and sleep on top of the three or four people sitting on it watching the movie. It became wildly popular and, to this day, I miss it. But guests started taking up time before the movie to promote an upcoming event or gallery opening or whatever, giving what amounted to a commercial. Then, too many people began showing up, people we didn't even know. Meanwhile, we had to upgrade our television set for the larger crowd. The previous set was rated PG, because all the colors were defaulting to pinks and greens.

One Monday evening, while Arlene and I were sitting down to eat dinner, someone rang the bell at our gate. I walked out and saw two expats, one holding a dish of food. I didn't know them.

“Is tonight Movie Night?” the woman asked.

I was thinking of asking who the hell they were; instead, I replied more civilly. “No. Movie Night is this Wednesday.”

The wife turned to her husband, as spouses do, and hit him on the arm. “See, I told you we should have called first.” They left but returned on Wednesday.

It was that kind of house. There was always—almost always—room at our inn.

The Seven Habits of Highly Effective Nuns

In my green and salad days, I was a card-carrying, cassock-wearing, dyed-in-the-wool, crucifix-waving, chest-beating, prayer-mumbling, hymn-singing, Rosary-bead-swinging Catholic. I attended parochial school through the eighth grade, wearing my uniform of white shirt, black pants, and black plastic shiny shoes with great shiny pride. I assisted at Mass as an altar boy during the Age of Confusion. Some of you may remember it as that pre-Vatican II epoch when you couldn't eat a cheeseburger on Friday without fear of eternal damnation and you had to memorize Latin without knowing what any of it meant.

To this day I can bow my head, tap my chest reverently, and recite the *Suscípiat*, the long passage that begins "*Suscípiat Dóminus sacrifícium de mánibus túis*" to anyone in a bar willing to buy me a drink.

I was chosen Altar Boy of the Year for my school for assisting at mass for nearly every day that year. It was before the internet and I had little else to do. As my reward, the school treated me to a semi-professional hockey game where

I was given an official hockey stick by the team. My brother and I used the hockey stick all summer long to snag peaches from a tree in our neighbor's backyard.

During an intensely spiritual five-day stretch that same year, after reading Father Butler's classic work *The Lives of the Saints*, a book about how saints suffer in defense of their faith, I took a vow of silence and refused to talk to anyone, including my parents.

Mom: He's not talking to me.

Dad: What's wrong?

Mom: I don't know. He hasn't said one word. Not one word. All day. Not a word.

Dad: Why won't you talk to your mother?

Awkward silence.

Dad: Maybe he's sick?

Mom: Do you think he's sick?

Dad: No. He's not sick. He's just being weird. Are you being weird?

I was being weird, and I was sorry. But I couldn't break my vow of silence, not even for my parents. I stood at the edge of a slippery slope. If I were to break my vow, the next step would be sniffing airplane glue, robbing liquor stores, getting caught doing both, and spending five-to-ten engaged to some bald guy with tats, body piercings and bad breath named Ike, Mike, Spike, or Pike. Besides, a vow is sacred—unless, of course, you're in politics.

Dad: Talk to me. Say something.
Mom: He won't answer. He's not talking to you, either.

It was perhaps the first time in the history of the Roman Catholic Church that a saint had his television privileges revoked and was sent to bed without his supper. Thus is the pious stuff martyrs are made of.

I attended Holy Family Catholic School in Citrus Heights, California, in what could best be described as an early bilingual educational experiment. The nuns spoke Spanish. The students spoke English. And miscommunication reigned supreme. It was a new school and the nuns were all from Latin America. We considered it their long-awaited payback for Teddy Roosevelt's big stick policy. Their big stick happened to be a 12-inch ruler.

In spite of the occasional knuckle-wrapping, the worst form of punishment I suffered was whenever two nuns would take turns shaking me by my collar while rattling off Spanish to each other at the lethal rate of five-thousand words a minute. In such moments I knew I was a goner. I expected the hairy, smoldering claw of Satan to break through the cement floor, snag me around the legs, and pull me to the fire and brimstone fate I so justly deserved. I felt sorry for my mother. She'd arrive at 3:30 that afternoon at school to pick me up and I wouldn't be there.

The nuns were pure sugar compared to the parish priest, Father Moretti. A tall, broad-shouldered Italian-American weaned on the streets of Brooklyn, Father Moretti was, in

a word, tough. His powerful voice could make grown men shake. His angry glare could shatter mighty souls into bits of nothingness. His use of language was colorful in the way that a longshoreman's vocabulary had spunk. We believed Father Moretti could put the fear of God in God.

High Mass, although rarely performed today, was the opera of my Catholic childhood. It involved pageantry, loud singing and seemed interminable, running forever without an intermission. The priest, decked out in his most elegant vestments, would parade around the inside of the church, swinging a brass incense burner as if trying to qualify for the hammer toss. With bowed head, assistants followed, carrying lighted candles. Someone played the organ and everybody sang, while in the loft above us mysterious voices chanted "Gloria in excelsis deo."

In short, a High Mass was and is very theatrical. But the key role, second only to that of the priest, was assigned to a deacon, who would follow the priest, step by step, while holding something that looked like an umbrella over the priest's head. The significance of the umbrella always baffled me since it rarely rained inside our church and lightning, contrary to my wishes, never struck.

But there he was one Sunday, my own father, playing the role of deacon, dressed in a cassock and holding that umbrella thing, as he walked behind Father Moretti, who chanted, sang, prayed, and swung incense with a vengeance. Unfortunately, my dad was much shorter than the tall priest and the umbrella kept banging into the back of Father

Moretti's head. You could almost hear the sound effect of each collision. In my mind I was watching a reenactment of a cartoon from the pages of *Mad Magazine*. THWACK! KREEEK! KA-THUNK! With each bump, the priest would grimace and look annoyed. At one point, Father Moretti had had enough, stopped singing in mid-lyric, turned and said to my father loud enough for all to hear: "Watch what the hell you're doing!" My dad backed off and left a comfortable space between himself and Father Moretti, making the umbrella more implied than applied.

But it is in the nature of the Catholic priest to forgive, as well as to seek charity. Within months, Father Moretti asked, once again, for my father's help. A new movie was showing at a local theater and Father Moretti was excited to see it. The good father was a good New Yorker and, of course, did not drive, so he asked my good father to take him. I tagged along.

The film was about a street-smart priest living in Brooklyn. A parishioner suggested it could be about Father Moretti's own early years, so off we went one evening to the Tower Theater, an art deco building on Main Street in nearby Roseville.

The film opened with great promise. We watched as a man in his early thirties was boxing in the ring, getting the better of his opponent. The film cut to the locker room where we watched the same man, now showered and dressed, put on his cleric's collar. We followed the priest as he walked through his own slice of Brooklyn, clearly well-known and

respected. People greeted him as he passed by: "How ya doing, Fah-thur?"... "Morning, Fah-thur"... "Smack anybody today, Fah-thur?"

The priest paused on the street in front of his rectory, the church standing tall and holy next to it. After a beat, the priest opened the gate and entered. The camera zoomed in for a close-up of the sign in front: "Saint John's Episcopal Church."

As if sitting on a launched booster rocket, Father Moretti shot out of his seat and shouted at the big screen, "He's a damn Episcopalian!" The disappointed priest stormed out of the theater, banging into knees and apologizing as he headed for the door. My father and I followed behind, closely on his heels.

Killing Them Softly with Paperclips

It's a beautiful day in the neighborhood in San Miguel, even more so than usual. The sky is robin egg's blue, the sun slowly warming like a stovetop on simmer, the air fresher than usual from last night's rain—and the dust, well, the dust is still present but, for the moment, it is less intrusive. So, in a nutshell and out of it, life is good. Small birds chirp in chorus while a handful of dogs join in and bark their refrain. Somewhere a rooster crows, a child's laughter can be heard. Over on the next street a car alarm suddenly goes off and just as suddenly stops broadcasting its warning. I sit in my interior courtyard and sip my second cup of coffee, a delicious organic brew from Chiapas, glowing from satisfaction and smiling. I stand, stretch, take another sip, and tell myself, "Today is the day I kill an expat."

Before you call the police, let me explain. In the crazy quilt world of my imagination, each adult receives a set of 100 commit-a-murder-for-free cards—or marbles or buttons or pebbles or whatever amulet or magical unit of measurement one chooses to use throughout life. In my case, I selected paperclips as my magic bullets. Paperclips are lighter than

marbles and take up less space than buttons. And, accordingly, I received my initial set of 100 clips back in the day. The only exception is New York City, where adults start with a base of 1,000 deadly talismans, and can renew up to three times. The rest of us only get 100 and must use them wisely. That might sound unfair to many of you, but have you ever lived in New York? I rest my case. Don't get me wrong. I love New York and I love expats. In fact, full disclosure, I am an expat, one of many in this town, and I've been to New York on many occasions and look forward to returning.

The population of expats in San Miguel, consisting mostly of Americans and Canadians, is currently estimated at between 10,000 and 15,000, out of an overall population of 160,000, including surrounding villages. These are all *mas o menos* guesses. It's a moving target since the number of expats in this town fluctuates depending on time of year: in winter, they are known as "snow birds" and in summer, as "sweat birds." Whatever the actual number or bird name, expats have historically made and continue to make a huge, positive difference in the community. For example, there are approximately 90 NGOs and charities in San Miguel, many of which are managed and supported by expats.

Expat charity extends beyond organizations and is often more personal and individual: rescuing stray dogs and cats, donating coats and blankets during winter, feeding the hungry, teaching English to children, providing educational scholarships to young adults living in the *campo*. The list goes on. Expats also help the local economy by hiring workers, frequenting restaurants, buying at stores great and small. You get the picture.

Then why do I want to kill an expat? I'm glad you asked. Let me start by saying I do not commit a murder literally, only metaphorically. It's less messy that way. When you feel like killing someone, you simply think of that person and throw away a marble or a button or, in my case, a paperclip. Boom. You're dead to me. Consider yourself clipped.

The good news is you will feel the same primitive, self-satisfied thrill of committing a necessary homicide for the greater good of Society or exacting revenge or teaching some buffoon a lesson and all without any of the associated legal costs or post-murder remorse. Of course, I tried other options first, including Haitian voodoo dolls, which turned out to be highly overrated and expensive. I tried giving them *Malocchio*, the Evil Eye, but people just turned away and avoided my glare. Or, in some cases, I forgot to remove my sunglasses first. I even tried the power of positive thinking. Another lesson learned. Apparently, the universe doesn't consider wishing someone dead to be a good use of positive energy, and my wishes were never met. Finally, I settled on the 100-personal talismans approach. So far, so good.

So, why kill an expat? Last week, my wife and I were having breakfast at a small restaurant in town, where we sat outside. An expat at the adjacent table was on her mobile phone and chatting, unaware that her unleashed dog had just defecated in front of another table, where another woman was eating her breakfast. This was not one of those restaurant

stories where either of us said, "I'll have what she's having." Instead, we told the woman on the phone about her dog. Eventually, she ended her conversation and picked up what her dog had left as a twenty-percent tip.

On our way home, during that same day, we passed another dog-owning expat on a mobile phone. Although her dog was leashed, the dog took advantage of waiting for its master to finish talking and did what is often referred to as a number two. Right there, mid-conversation, on the ground, at her feet. The expat moved slightly away from it and continued talking. Clearly, she chose to ignore the excrement and had no intention of picking it up. I looked at the woman and pleaded "Lady!" so many times I began to sound like Jerry Lewis. Still on her phone, the expat walked away, leaving her dog's deposit behind on the sidewalk.

The next day, Arlene and I were walking in *Centro*, the historic district, on our way to pick up our mail. Two men and one woman, all Americans, walked in front of us. One of the men pulled their dog on a leash. The dog pulled back on the leash and defecated in the middle of the street. The man looked at the dog and asked why it did that? He looked unsuccessfully for something to use to pick up the mess, gave up after three seconds of intense effort and shrugged. The other two said to just leave it and they continued on their way.

Don't blame the dog, buddy. It's a simple rule: walk a dog, bring a bag, pick it up. In fact, that's the entire point of taking a dog out for a walk. If a dog could use the toilet in your house, he'd never see the outside world. But when a dog has got to go, he's got to go. It's not as if your dog can hold out for the men's room at the Marriott.

As much as I wanted to paperclip those scofflaws, I didn't. When you use one of your fatal talismans on someone, you lose it forever, leaving you with one less in your Quiver of Justice. And because life can be longer than expected, I've always been frugal with my paperclips. That is, until the Trump presidency, during which time I exhausted a large portion of my stash at an insane pace. Don't get me started. Which means, sadly, I am down to my last four paperclips and didn't want to spend any of my remaining stash on those particular expats. Still, I hate it when expats move here or tourists visit the beautiful, colonial town of San Miguel, and treat it like a garbage can. This town deserves better; Mexico and Mexicans deserve better; we all deserve better.

Which begs the question: what happens when you lose all your marbles or, in my case, paperclips? Well, pard, I'm afraid it's game over. But—and here's the real beauty of my murderous scheme—when you're out of talismans, you are forced to accept people just as they are. You can't kill them anymore, metaphorically, so you might as well learn to live with them, literally. Live and let live, I say. Different strokes for different folks. Be open-minded. Be more forgiving. Start quoting the Dali Lama and sing along with the Mormon Tabernacle Choir in a rousing rendition of *Ode to Joy.*

Unless, of course, you live in New York.

Who or What's Buried at the Ponderosa Ranch?

When people in the U.S. find out we live in Mexico, they always ask the same three questions. Is it safe? What do you do for health care? And what's on TV? Because of the first two questions I'm not sure how much time I have left in life, so I think it's a good idea to prioritize and tackle the most important question first: namely, our TV viewing options.

We have plenty. Our standard cable package includes in excess of 80 channels, and, as in the USA, most of those channels are filled with spouses screaming at each other, boring community board meetings, and the same sexy woman who appears just about everywhere in the world, wearing a tiny bikini and showing viewers how to tighten their abs. For bonus points, we have about a dozen channels featuring professional soccer games and you can always find at least one *lucha libre* match, where portly men wear Halloween masks and spandex tights as they take turns throwing each other around an elevated canvas mat. And if that's not exciting enough for you, there are always the *telenovelas*, the much shorter soap opera Latin cousin of *The Young & The Restless.*

To put it another way, our television viewing habits have changed but only slightly.

Take, for example, the channel that serves as our online TV Guide. A similar channel in the U.S. enabled us to scroll back and forth quickly to see what's ahead on a particular channel. Our online TV Guide in Mexico scrolls, unfortunately, at a leisurely pace, one might even suggest at the pace of a donkey, and often does not allow us to see beyond one hour ahead with any precision. They merely list that an upcoming show will be from the U.S. but it doesn't tell you which show.

But I quibble. Because of our slow-moving virtual TV Guide, we developed a prioritized process of channel surfing as a substitute. When clicking through the channels, we first decide if a show is in English; if it is, then it's often reason enough for us to stop right there. This has resulted in unusual and surprising viewing pleasures, from duck hunting to specific techniques of beading.

If a show has subtitles in Spanish, there's a good chance the voices on the show are in English. The only time this theory lets us down is when we reach The European Channel, where the spoken language is likely to be German with Spanish subtitles.

Much like how they keep old Detroit beater cars from the 50s and 60s running, Mexico is also keeping old USA television shows alive and well. My favorite is what I call the "Bonanza" channel. It's in the middle of the channel crowd and runs the old Western show starring Ben Cartwright and sons seemingly around the clock—and in Spanish. Have you

ever taken a good look at those three boys? Adam, Hoss, Little Joe? They don't look anything like their father. So, I'm guessing there once was a ranch hand named Big Joe who was pretty handy with a lasso and branding iron.

Curiosity got the better of me one afternoon, and I did a little research and learned that the three boys all had different mothers. By the time the series began, all those moms had died. Hmm. Which begs the question, who or what's buried on "The Ponderosa" besides fir trees?

Watching shows in Spanish with English subtitles—or English with Spanish subtitles—is an excellent way to improve one's foreign language skills. But it has its limits. In an English-speaking show, for instance, when a character, usually male and usually in a violent scene, wildly drops the F-bomb as if he were carpet bombing a conversational jungle, the polite Spanish subtitle shakes its head in dismay, waves a disapproving finger, and writes "*maldición*." Or, in other words, "bad word."

I love that aspect about Mexico, the politeness and awareness of others in the room. Unfortunately, if you find yourself in a heated argument in Spanish down here, I doubt repeatedly shouting "*maldición*" at your opponent will get you anywhere.

Of course, all of this could be avoided by paying extra for a satellite dish that runs Canadian channels. A channel devoted to Curling? Sign me up.

Well, that was TV viewing in good old San Miguel during our first time here as local residents. Today, cable providers in town offer everything you can get north of the border, including premium services such as Netflix and Amazon, even if what's offered has been slightly tailored or restricted. The catch is, these shows run on Mexican time, which means you're never quite sure when they will really start. Some of the shows are reruns of reruns, soccer is on twenty-four hours a day, and if they're showing a movie from Poland, all the subtitles will be in Spanish.

All in all, not bad. Still, who wants to stay inside and watch television when you're surrounded by so much beauty and history in a town full of stories?

Ten Things I Don't Understand About You

As an American expat living full-time in San Miguel, I am often confused. I admit that some of my confusion while living here can be traced back to a lack of cultural insights or historical understanding on my part. For that, I openly apologize. But there are other aspects of living here that still baffle me, even after several years. Although I have limited my list to ten, I assure you my confusion knows no bounds. Nonetheless, confusion is a small price to pay for living in the best city in the world. Without further ado, here are my top ten head-scratchers:

Chalk marks on houses

We all see it. We all see it. I know I've seen them. Small markings in chalk like a game of tic-tac-toe, filled in with a mix of letters and numbers, scrawled on the wall outside of a house. Have these houses been targeted for some kind of special treatment from the local government? Or, maybe, could it be a sign right out of the Bible offering safety from governmental retribution? What's to stop others from erasing the chalk? And what happens to the message when a heavy rain falls? Are these symbols explained somewhere and posted for all to see? Perhaps these exist as shorthand explanations of the cryptic Aztec calendar or some touristy scribbles by extraterrestrials? It's an unsolved mystery, and I don't get it. I just don't get it.

Replacing stones in the street

I know and appreciate the need for the city to provide employment. I wholly get that and I totally support that. What I don't get is how they determine which stones in a cobblestoned street are defective and must be replaced? Is there a Minister of Faulty Cobblestones who wanders around the town pointing to stones that are past their prime, followed closely in his steps by a lower-ranked official taking notes? These are stones, rocks, and pebbles, my friends, not trees suffering from Oak Wilt or Diplodia tip blight. I can understand the obvious need to replace stones if the earth somehow opened up like a Florida sinkhole and started swallowing entire buses. But, quite frankly, I am unable to determine a good stone from a bad stone, which probably says more about a lack of discernment on my part. Fortunately, San Miguel has many discerning experts well-trained in the arcane craft of stone sorting.

Generic pharmacies

There's no shortage of generic pharmacies in San Miguel known as *farmacias similares*. When you consider the average age of the average expat, a glut of pharmacies is actually a good thing. These shops are everywhere and enjoy a low-barrier of entry. Just bring in an empty bottle or packet of

something and they'll fill it—with something, anything, no doctor's prescription needed. Plus, whatever they give you is often cheaper than what you paid for in the original. And therein lies the rub. How do I know with any certainty that I am walking out of the store with the real thing, albeit under an undecipherable brand label? Likewise, how do I know I won't be taking pills for toe fungus when I believe I am taking my heart medication? Then again, how do I know with certainty the same problem doesn't exist in the States? I guess this one is a wash.

Small dusty-white poodles

You might think the Chihuahua would be San Miguel's town dog, and you'd be wrong. Small white dogs, mostly poodle in breed but with other breeds thrown in to make guessing more enjoyable, are everywhere. Collectively they are known as The San Miguel Special. They clearly outnumber Chihuahuas. Where do these mixes come from? My guess is that twice a year a circus rolls through town and performing male poodles sow their oats in a wild week of no-regret sex. Poodles gone wild. The Chihuahuas, on the other hand, are practicing safe sex.

Street house numbers

This one defies logic. If you've walked around town looking for a specific house, you have most likely already experienced this problem first-hand. House numbers are often not in sequential order and sometimes the same exact address is given to two different houses next to or far apart from each other. When we lived on Stirling Dickinson, our address was the same—to the number and letter—as a house at the opposite end of the street. I understand when street numbering may be abruptly broken because of a dead-end only to reopen a few houses later. That said, we've struggled to find the correct address more than once because there was more than one house with the same address assigned to it. Color me puzzled.

Melting ice

This is another one that doesn't make much sense and leaves me totally confused. On our morning walks into *Centro,* we start by leaving our house and cross over to *Calzada de Aurora.* Usually, our walks begin sometime between 9 A.M. and 10 A.M., with the actual time varying. What doesn't vary—or hasn't varied so far—is this puzzlement: three huge blocks of ice melt in front of a small store that hasn't opened yet. Instead of asking the delivery of their ice to be made later or an employee to show up earlier, the owner simply lets the ice melt, and it does. We watched in anticipation one morning as a dog sniffed the ice and waited for the curious dog in the day to lift its leg. It didn't, I am pleased to report. Although melting ice is a singular example, we notice other examples during our walks through town of not thinking things through or what I classify as being unclear on the concept. Consider this example a metaphor for a larger problem.

Images of Our Lady of Guadalupe

Our Lady of Guadalupe, also known as the Virgin of Guadalupe, is the *numero uno* saint in Mexico. She is

revered religiously and is a source of national pride. The novelist Carlos Fuentes said, "You cannot truly be considered a Mexican unless you believe in the Virgin of Guadalupe." I'm okay with that; raised as a Catholic, I understand the powerful pull of the saints and their associated imagery. What I don't understand is why just about any image of the Virgin plastered or painted on a house or building will serve to prevent graffiti and reduce crime. Yet the mere images seem to work, even better than a rooftop dog or a high-tech security system. Which begs the question, if I wear a shirt with Our Lady of Guadalupe's image on it, will that protect me from getting mugged late at night? Hmm. TBD.

Passing cars

You would think that the first car behind a slow car would be the first to pass, and after it, the second car in line, and so on, ahem, down the line, in some sort of civilized order. In actual practice, it doesn't quite work that way, as far as I can tell. Based on a mysterious mental algorithm, drivers in Mexico at the end of a line feel entitled to be the first car to hit the passing lane. It defies both common sense and the laws of risk management, but it may explain why most cars have a set of rosary beads dangling from their rear-view mirror.

Church bells

They chime, they ring, they do their thing. At all hours and relentlessly. I actually don't mind the sound of church bells ringing and, in fact, find it charming. I just don't understand why they ring when they do or for how long.

Sometimes they ring on the hour or half-hour, other times at seven minutes after or twenty minutes before. I give up. It's similar to the scheduling of TV shows on cable here. Instead of a show beginning at, say, eight, it actually starts at seven-forty-eight or eight-ten. This is a corollary to the Mexican Time concept, where a plumber agrees to show up tomorrow at two in the afternoon but doesn't show up for three days later and at, you guessed it, two P.M. Time may not stand still in this town, but it certainly marches to a different clock, mixed metaphor notwithstanding.

You're always so friendly

Perhaps my greatest confusion is in this category. After all the racist anti-Mexican crap spewed by certain misguided Americans north of the border in the United States, you seem to still love us. You don't blame us personally. Defying all vindictive odds, you remain gracious and courteous and welcoming. When we meet on the street, you wish us to have a good day; when you see us in a restaurant, you wish us to have a good meal. Your language is beautiful; your smiles uplifting. If we need a helping hand, you're always there extending it. My reaction this time is a happy confusion. Thank you for allowing us to live in your beautiful country and to be your neighbor.

The Doctor Will See You Now

Whenever we return to visit friends and relatives in the United States, we are always asked two questions: is Mexico safe and what do you do for medical care? I finally figured an easy way to answer both questions with the same reply. I tell them we'll probably be kidnapped or killed before the year is out, so medical care isn't an issue.

People who know me will roll their eyes or purse their lips, some might chuckle and shake their head. On the other hand, the mouths of people who don't know me will usually drop wide open or they'll flash me that "I knew it" smile. Then I'll tell them, quickly, I was only joking. We've lived in Mexico full-time for more than eight years and can't imagine living anywhere else, which is why we keep returning.

We're ten hours by car from most of the violence in Mexico and feel safe. In fact, we made the six-day drive in our cramped car from Portland, Oregon, to San Miguel, arriving tired and dirty and smelly but relatively unscathed the first two times we moved here. In violation of such mainstream media expectations, we didn't get car-jacked, kidnapped, or mistakenly shot at.

Let's face it. We're all in the line of fire, no matter where we live. Someone walked into a hair salon in Seal Beach, California, and killed eight people. And a guy went berserk in Seattle at a coffee shop and killed five others before taking his own life. According to FBI crime statistics, Mexico is twice as safe for Texans than Texas (and three times safer than Houston).

As one Mexican government official pointed out: "There are more than 2,500 municipalities in Mexico, and the majority of violence is in 12 of them." Or as journalist Linda Ellerbee said in an essay on the topic, "Talking about drug violence in Mexico without naming a state or city where this is taking place is rather like looking at the horror of Katrina and saying, 'Damn. Did you know the U.S. is under water?'"

Medical care is another matter. First, some background. I'm in the VA system, which, I might add, is wonderful and I think everyone should be so lucky. If I need any major medical care, I'll return to the U.S. and seek it.

However, for my day-to-day medical care south of the border, I have a regular physician here in town. The cost of a visit is about 800 pesos, *más o menos*, which at the current exchange rate is about forty dollars—so it's less than my old co-pay under a company-provided medical plan when I was a worker-bee in high tech. My doctor is a conventional physician, fully trained, tri-lingual, and not an obvious advocate of, say, alternative medicine. (There's nothing wrong with the alternative path and plenty of people are happy to follow it here in San Miguel). I don't have to wait long to

see my doctor, and he spends as much time as he thinks he needs. In short, it's not conveyor belt medical treatment with the doctor playing Beat the Clock.

Additionally, many medications are cheaper here than in the United States and it seems as if there's either a regular pharmacy or a generic-brands pharmacy on every street corner. For example, I have asthma. One time upon returning to the U.S. I checked on renewing my inhaler. Because I didn't have a medical plan that included drug coverage, it was going to cost me $200 for the refill. Now I could get the same inhaler in Mexico for the equivalent of between $30 and $40—and that's without any kind of medical plan.

San Miguel has two hospitals, one private and the other public. However, we're 30 minutes by car from a hospital in another city and, traveling in a different direction, one hour by car from major U.S.-style hospitals that are as modern as they come. In 2021, local city officials discussed the opportunity to invest in more medical care here and make San Miguel a medical-vacation stop. There are insurance plans one can purchase to help cover medical care in Mexico, but those tend to be expensive and come with high deductibles. There's another insurance program available that will cover your air flight to the U.S. or Canada for medical care and back again, spouse included. To recap, most of our medical needs can be met locally, and if they can't, we plan to return north as needed.

Our primary health concern upon returning to San Miguel, was, of course, the pandemic. Like many expats living here, we were fortunate to not have to go to work. As a result, we hunkered down in our house, masked up every day whenever we went out, ordered the occasional meal in and groceries delivered, kept the recommended social distance from other people when out and about and avoided, as they say, like the plague, crowds and close interiors. We were never without a mask. In fact, one night I took off my mask and Arlene screamed. Budda bing. Rim shot.

Once vaccines became available, a few of our expat friends traveled to the United States to get their shot. Let's face it, for a while there, the U.S. was just as confused about getting the vaccine out to the masses as other countries, with the possible exceptions of New Zealand and Israel.

We elected to stay in San Miguel and see what Mexico had to offer. It was not easy waiting, and we had to live through a series of false rumors: we would be getting the Sputnik vaccine (okay); we'd be getting the Chinese vaccine (less okay). Quite frankly, I was ready to take any vaccine and didn't care if it came from Malta or from Make Glorious Vaccine by Glorious Nation of Kazakhstan. As it turned out, we were to receive the Pfizer vaccine, which came from an American company but was developed by the German biotechnology company BioNTech.

Standing in a long line was our best option, the government rightly concluded. Making an appointment through your local pharmacy wouldn't work, because of an insufficient supply of those businesses. Besides, expats would show up early for their appointment and Mexicans would show up

late and the schedule would be off track from the opening bell. Chaos would reign supreme.

One Monday, we were told to be prepared to get our first shot the following morning, and even told where to go for the injection. By that same Monday afternoon, however, it was called off. Thursday, same week, we were told the vaccination program in San Miguel would start the next day, Friday, running from 8 A.M. to 8 P.M. The anti-Covid brigade would be at one of more than a dozen sites across town. Fortunately, a site was a short walk from our house, and that's where we went at seven in the morning. The line was already long, and we were issued numbers 187 and 188. We waited all day, first in the shade and then in the glaring sun and then back in the shade. It took six and a half hours to get our first shot. We eventually clocked out and were home before 4 P.M.

Three weeks later, we were told on a Monday that the second shot would be available the next day, Tuesday, again from eight in the morning until eight at night. We were told to return to where we received our first shot and wait our turn. We arrived at 6:30 A.M., thinking we would snag a better place in line, only to see the line much longer than before. We were further back this time and held numbers 279 and 280. After many hours, mostly spent under the unforgiving eye of a cheerful sun, we made it through the front gate of the clinic, had our paperwork approved, and were waved on to the "shot" office. That's when our game plan went awry, much like the best laid plans of mice and bureaucrats: they needed to do a shift change and decided to shut down their operation for nearly an hour. So close, yet so far. All in all, we spent nine hours waiting in line for the second shot.

But, here again, our story has a happy ending. Thanks to the hard work and commitment of so many healthcare workers and volunteers in San Miguel, we had been vaccinated twice and were a mere two weeks away from being street legal.

We tend to live a healthier life in the mountain town of San Miguel de Allende, six thousand feet above sea level. We're outside a lot. We walk just about everywhere we go (when we had a car, we would put ten dollars' worth of gas in the car every six weeks). All our produce is local and mostly organic and, I might add, cheap and delicious. Plus, we're more relaxed. We're no longer commuting and stuck in traffic, stewing in our juices and watching both the car's thermostat and our own blood pressures rise.

Oh, I almost forgot. The doctors here make house calls and the pharmacies make home deliveries. Sweet.

I've Grown Accustomed to Your Pollen

It's spring in beautiful downtown San Miguel, when a young man's fancy turns to many things, especially sneezing. I am no longer a young man but I have what's known as the trifecta of histamines racing through my body at various times of the year: allergies, asthma, and atopic dermatitis. Put another way, if I were a three-headed creature from the Greek underworld made by Disney, I'd been known as Sneezy, Wheezy, and Scratchy.

Since moving to the middle of Mexico, my wife, Arlene, has seen her allergies explode. Every March, when the drop-dead gorgeous purple jacaranda trees are in bloom, she sneezes with wild abandon. I imagine one could sneeze with mild abandon but I have yet to see it. Thus, our house in San Miguel, a city known for its flowers, has become a flower-free zone. For two months every year, we shake our fists and curse the beautiful but blooming *jacarandas*.

According to at least one common theory, allergies are a dated flaw in the design of the human body. When the body's immune system detects a mostly harmless allergen as life-threatening, some mechanism in charge somewhere deep inside the body shouts, "Release the nistamines" and that's when the fun starts. Cue the sneezing, wheezing, coughing, scratching, weepy eyes, many sleepless nights and more than one trip to a local doctor's office. Different bodies react differently to allergens, however, and the event can prove life-threatening for some, a mere annoyance for others.

Allergies. Can't live with 'em, can't live without 'em. We're told the best defense is to avoid irritants, yet we're surrounded by them. Grass. Tree pollen. Weed pollen. Dust mites. Mold. Smoke of any kind. The three poisons: ivy, oak, sumac. Jewelry. Household chemicals. Perfume. Rubber. Nickel. Cotton. Wool. Bees from every nest. Yellow jackets, hornets, and wasps. Just about any other winged thing, not to mention ants representing every anthill on earth. Aspirin. Penicillin. Shellfish. Eggs. Milk. Grains. Peanuts. Other nuts, you choose. Berries. Dogs. Cats. Hamsters.

The human body is still home to several internal components that once served a purpose and are now considered vestigial or mostly useless, like an anatomical lava lamp or selfie stick or all those VHS tapes you're still carrying around but don't know why. Best known among those genetic garage sale hand-me-downs is, of course, the appendix (removed when I was seven) and the coccyx or tailbone (sitting on it now). I think the generous release of histamines by the body's immune system in reaction to what it perceives as a lethal invasion—but is not—might qualify as something left over from those wild pathogen keggers held during the Paleolithic Age. A key difference is that while an allergic reaction can kill you, mostly what happens when you sit in front of a computer for long periods of time is gain weight. Now that I think about it, sitting too long in front of a computer can kill you as well. So, there we are: we're screwed, blued, and tattooed every which way from Sunday.

If you have not already guessed, I am not a doctor and this is not a how-to essay on dealing with allergies or about the ontological proof of IgE. In my experience, allergies are like distant cousins. They can appear in your life at any time and surprise you by going away on their own without much fanfare. Here today, gone tomorrow. Or maybe not.

I wanted to discuss the allergy scene in San Miguel, however. But first, I'm going to digress further and present my credentials as someone who has always had to deal with an over-active immune system.

When I was a child with asthma, one of the preferred oral medications for treating an asthma attack was Tedral, a theophylline-based drug. It was so powerful that I could only take one half of a tablet and had to sit or try to lie down while my legs would shake in reaction. Today, if experiencing a flare up of my asthma I might take a corticosteroid, such as Prednisone, for about a week or until my chest returns to normal. Life's full of tradeoffs, so when I take Prednisone my breathing eases but my cheeks puff up like Rocky the Squirrel and my mood swings back and forth more times than a ping pong ball in Beijing. I've had every major treatment for asthma known to allergists and pulmonologists alike, from desensitization shots to steam tents, and occasionally still a tightness reigns in my chest. For reasons unknown to me, my asthma became dormant from about age 20 until I was in my late-30s, when it came back with a vengeance and an I.O.U. It has since shown no signs of leaving anytime soon.

Along with the big wheeze, I suffer from an allergy-induced dry skin condition known as eczema. It's not quite the heartbreak of psoriasis of Madison Avenue fame but it has its own challenges. As a kid, I had to take sponge baths or, worse still, bathe in starch or oatmeal. You might think a starch bath for a kid would be pretty cool and leave him with arms stuck out like Frankenstein groping his way down the hall. But the sad truth is I couldn't stay in the tub long enough to get a good starch going and it wouldn't matter anyway because I had to cover my skin in some kind of lubricant once I exited the tub. I could rarely relax because I was constantly scratching. When I lived in Reno, Nevada, my skin, at times, became so parched and caked I could barely move my neck from one side to the other. On the other hand, when I lived in Portland, Oregon, my skin was always moist and smooth, but the cold, damp weather of the Willamette Valley triggered many an asthma attack. What's a mere mortal to do?

Besides my weak lungs and sensitive skin, I have hay fever, and a host of irritants, from pet dander to seasonal pollen; a sudden drop in barometric pressure can be enough to launch a sneezing fit. I could go on but we all have our tales of biological woe. Besides, I wanted to tell you about how my histamines are enjoying life in the sunny colonial highlands of Mexico.

The short answer is they're doing fine, which surprises me because according to an ancient skin-scratch test I took as a kid, a test considered a Rorschach for allergists, I am especially allergic to dust and dust is San Miguel's unofficial nickname. If money could be made selling dust, it would be the town's leading export. Yet even with all the dust, smoke, and unidentified particulate matter floating around here at the six-thousand-foot level, my breathing is the best it has been in years. My skin, too, has improved and only erupts during the very dry months of April and May. Sneezing still happens but infrequently.

In conclusion, I submit of all the places I've lived, from northern California to northern Oregon, from Nevada to Puerto Rico to a small island in the middle of the Indian Ocean, the semi-arid mountain town of San Miguel de Allende, Mexico, offers the most beneficial climate for the various histamines that haunt me. And that's nothing to be sneezed at.

Holy Pozole

Good evening. I am truly honored to be here tonight and to have been asked by my host to say a few words about the food in San Miguel.

As Mark's stomach, I'm his fifth favorite body organ. Stomachs are normally not credited with many insights. We growl or rumble to get attention, otherwise we pretty much go unrecognized. Indeed, in any hierarchy among human body parts, a stomach rarely ranks in the top five. We're considered too emotional, I am told, driven mostly by appetite and smells and other visceral reactionary habits, as if there's something wrong with that. They say we're more instinctive than rational and to that I say so what — instinct could be much older than reason. Who knows for sure?

But, if there is one thing I know with certainty, it is my way around food, so when my host said we were moving back to San Miguel de Allende, Mexico, I was elated. San Miguel is called the "Heart of Mexico" but it could just as easily be called the "Stomach of Mexico." Allow me to explain.

Stomachs are rarely afforded much recognition. Sure, people often say someone doesn't have the stomach for

omething (*hello, if they have a stomach, it is for something*) or they have butterflies in their stomach (*preposterous; how'd they get in there, a butterfly eating contest?*) or it made my stomach turn (*spoiler alert, I'm turning all the time*). And my personal favorite: he has a sensitive stomach. So what? Can't I be sensitive just like, say, the heart or colon? Sensitivity in a heart is considered admirable but apply it to your stomach and suddenly it's a negative trait and you're gobbling antacids. Like that's fair? I mean who decided gastro-intestinal matters were no better than a gut check?

Sorry.... Deep breath. Exhale. Deep breath. Exhale. Count to ten.... Okay, I'm ready to continue. I apologize for sounding so defensive in my opening remarks. I'm told one should never start a speech with an apology. But I'm still in therapy, you see, and it's a work in progress and there's some lingering resentment and so on and so forth. I guess what I'm trying to say is it's not easy being a stomach.

As a stomach, there was much I sacrificed by moving back to Oregon, with the huge exception of Dungeness crab, which I would kinda-sorta kill for and is easy to find in Oregon but nowhere to be found in the middle of Mexico. Above the border, I missed and craved the authentic tortilla chips available in San Miguel, crispy-fried in lard and as thick as a plate. Unlike those paper-thin, pre-packaged, mass-produced tortilla chips available in every store in the U.S., you can use the chips down here with salsa, guacamole, *pico de gallo*, and any other kind of dip without fear of dripping on the carpet. In fact, my favorite new discovery the last time I lived here was *Chilaquiles*, a corn tortilla dish that answered the age-old question of what to do with day-old nachos. I also missed the amazing Mexican wedding cookies, a sublime version of a round shortbread cookie covered in powered sugar, as well as the incredible almond or chocolate croissants available at most bakeries in town. I could devour such croissants every hour of the day, but ultimately it would be bad form. Although a stomach can be enthusiastic in its desires, it also must show a modicum of restraint. Otherwise, a stomach can easily become too big for its own britches. It's basic Stomach 101 and a sad fact of the human anatomy.

Truth be told, this is one stomach who was very happy to return to San Miguel. Walking through the same streets as before, the aroma of tacos and tamales and grilled corn wafted toward me like an old friend, triggering my juices with delight. Restaurants tempted me as I walked by, offering Italian or Peruvian or German or Asian or Indian or, yes, Mexican dishes. Freshly ground coffee from Oaxaca or Chiapas or Veracruz hangs in the air. Fresh fruits and vegetables abound on street corners and in tiendas, from local farms to the nearest table; egg yolks so brightly yellow they look like miniature suns; chicken moles as complex and mystical as the Aztec religion itself. Excuse me. I'm beginning to wax poetic, I'm afraid.

Granted, stomachs are not known for their poetry or spirituality. In fact, we're generally known for the opposite trait: we're considered base or coarse, all appetite and no

refinement. However, this time around I believe I may have finally reached a higher spiritual plane as a stomach and found true nirvana. I am referring to a Mexican dish called *Pozole*.

What is it? *Pozole* is a popular Mexican soup.

I know what you're thinking. Okay, is that it, is that all? A soup? Seriously? You might wonder how could I experience what amounts to a religious experience over a mere bowl of soup?

Let me start by telling you when it is cooking on the stove, your gastric juices start running through your system like histamines after a bee sting. As a stomach, I consider all these aromas to be foreplay for the big event. Its main ingredient is hominy, a kind of puffy corn strong enough to hold its consistency in soup. There are a ton of spices added, of course, because this is Mexican cuisine, and its main protein is either pork (my favorite) or chicken. There are three types of *Pozole*, depending on the chiles used: red, green, or white. It takes hours to cook and, while cooking, fills the stomach with so much joy you wouldn't believe. Insurmountable anticipation to the point of being giddy. Can I hear an Amen?

Is P*ozole* a new dish? Hardly. In fact, *Pozole* is probably as old as the Aztec empire, though initially without the pigs or chicken, which came much later. When it has been cooked and is ready for your stomach, you'll be able to add your choice of condiments to it: radish, green onion, cheese, sour cream, avocado, tortilla chips, etc.

I see my allotted time is almost up. If you've never experienced the joy of eating *Pozole*, I encourage you to try it.

And now, if you'll excuse me and there are no questions, there's a delicious bowl of *Pozole* with my name on it back stage. Enjoy the rest of your evening, my friends, and please do not take your stomach for granted. We all have a role to play in this life.

Oh, one more thing. I've been asked to remind everyone that next week the Small Intestine and Colon will be in conversation on this same stage about what happens to all this delicious food as it passes through me. I understand they'll be showing some very graphic images. It sounds riveting.

¡Buen provecho!

Yes, Scottie, there are Second Acts

After living in San Miguel de Allende, Mexico, the first time for two years, we moved back to the U.S. in 2007, turning right at Mexico's northern border, instead of left, and heading due east. We were moving to Asheville, North Carolina, where we had purchased a house online that was still under construction. We were guaranteed our new house would be finished and we would be able to move in shortly after arriving in Asheville.

I now know that shopping online has its limits and one should stick to what you can wear or listen to or put on a book shelf or in a microwave. Our house wasn't ready when we arrived and still wasn't ready three months later, two months after we relinquished rights to it. We eventually negotiated our way of the contract and returned to Portland. For at least three weeks in-between, however, we suffered through what was then the most humid August on record in Asheville. The four of us—two humans, one canine, one feline—stayed inside our motel room and hunkered down for best positioning in front of the air conditioner, elbowing and inching our way through each other like roller derby queens.

One of the few times Arlene and I left the air-chilled room was to visit Best Buy. We had purchased a Virgin mobile phone there earlier in the week but could not read the miniscule print in their getting started handout that identified our activation code. We boldly marched into Best Buy, indignant, righteous, ready to demand a refund and complain about the product and the ridiculously tiny print in the handbook.

How dare they! According to the authorities who measure such things, there are 72 points to an inch; the standard for reading is a size between 10 and 12 points. I considered the Virgin mobile phone activation code print to come in around a minus-6 on the points scale. We handed the phone to the young customer service representative. She looked at the start up instructions and quickly wrote the code on a piece of paper in large print and handed it back to me. I asked her if she wore contacts. She told me no. There was nothing wrong with her vision, she added. Humiliated, I took back our phone, grabbed Arlene, and we very slowly walked back to our car, ancient arm in ancient arm, not sure we'd reach the car before going totally blind or dying of old age in the store parking lot.

I was looking forward to living in Asheville, called the "Paris of the South." The small city features a wide range of impressive architectural styles, including many Art Deco buildings, saved from urban renewal demolition over the years because of the city's financial difficulties following the crash of 1929. Their financial pain was architecture's gain.

I was also intrigued by the city's literary history. North Carolina native William Sydney Porter ("O. Henry") is buried in the town's cemetery, as is Thomas Wolfe (*Look Homeward, Angel*). More recently, Charles Frazier, author of the National Book Award-winning novel *Cold Mountain*, is an Asheville native and, as of this writing, very much alive and well and not ready to be interred. But it's the F. Scott Fitzgerald linkage to Asheville that I wanted to talk about. You may recall the famous author of *The Great Gatsby* once said, "There are no second acts in American lives." San Miguel begs to differ.

When we returned to San Miguel in 2010, I made a vow to myself to get more involved in the local community, especially in the arts, to meet more people and become an active resident. After so many years of working regular jobs while squeezing in time to write or draw early in the morning or late at night, I was looking forward to flipping the cycle and spending much more time on creative interests and less time on day-to-day survival activities, such as hunting bison or harvesting corn.

In 2006, during our first stay, I attended the initial San Miguel Writers' Conference. The nascent event was small, with more volunteers than attendees. I worked as a door monitor, which meant I would stand near the door, make sure we had enough seats, check registrations, and remind the presenter how much time he or she had before the class ended. I was the None Shall Pass guard, arms crossed and eyes pinched. Put another way, I was a door knob on two legs, but unlike a door knob, I could also direct participants to the nearest bathroom. In my absence, the conference had taken off to become one of the better international writers' conferences on the circuit. So, after returning to San Miguel, it wasn't long before I volunteered again to help with the conference, only this time I was put in charge of what was known as the concurrent workshops, 90-minute classes, with morning and afternoon sessions, stretched over three and a half days. I was in charge of all the door monitors and rooms, which also meant, much to my chagrin, as they say in the chagrin business, I was in charge of the audio-visual equipment, mostly projectors connected to a presenter's computer.

True confession time. I was never the AV Guy in high school. In fact, I was the other frail, shy, short, skinny kid with thick eyeglasses and big ears and a runny nose. The crowning achievement of my high school freshman year was not getting stuffed in a locker. (I'm doing better now. Thanks for asking.)

The writers' conference was and remains, even during the recent pandemic, an incredible, almost magical event in a small city in the middle of Mexico. Normally, the conference takes place during the middle of February, but during 2020, in response to the pandemic, the conference became virtual and took advantage of online connectivity by extending their "literary season" to run from October 2020 through March 2021. In addition to an impressive list of keynote speakers and instructors over the years, the conference

brings together writers from everywhere—and many local volunteers help make it happen. San Miguel writers and writer wannabees experience at least one second act while living here. In earlier years, I also taught conference workshops and gave readings of my book, as did Arlene.

When writing *Nobody Knows the Spanish I Speak*, I struggled with how to define in a single sentence what appealed to me most about living in San Miguel as an American expat. At the risk of quoting myself, here's what I think I said: "You can't swing an artist in this town without hitting a writer, and if the writer ducks you're bound to hit a jazz musician." Or something along those lines. Maybe I'm misquoting myself. It's happened before.

My next Second Act came toward the end of 2012. I was discussing ten-minute plays with another writer, Michael Hager, and we realized the short theatrical form, a genre that's been around since the 1970s, was a perfect fit for the typical older expat audience in San Miguel, with their shorter attention spans and frequent need for more bathroom breaks. My favorite quote about the ten-minute play genre comes from Jon Jory, at the time a producer-director at Actors Theatre of Louisville and one of the format's earliest advocates: "A ten-minute play can tell a story that forty minutes or two hours would have ruined, and we've all gotten stuck with that guy at a party." Not knowing if audiences would be interested, we produced San Miguel's first international ten-minute play festival and called it *Diez Minutos*. I had no experience whatsoever producing plays; Michael, a published song writer, had been involved in the production of concerts. Although I had short plays produced, I was never involved in any of the productions. Nonetheless, we started *Diez Minutos* and, at least until it was shut down because of the pandemic, it ran for eight consecutive years, including four years after Michael and I had both left Mexico and were no longer the producers. The festival has remained in very capable and dedicated hands.

Back to the *Diez Minutos* origin story. Suddenly, I was a producer. I was in the same profession as the notorious Max Bialystock and Leo Bloom. Unlike Mr. Bialystock, however, our shows didn't close on the opening night of rehearsals, and unlike Mr. Bloom, I didn't want everything I'd ever seen in the movies. Okay, maybe a few things. Unsure if San Miguel audiences would be interested in plays only ten-minutes long, we made our inaugural event invitation-only and invited 50 playwrights from around the world to submit a play. They did. From that batch, we selected six plays; we also invited local playwrights to enter and reserved two spots for local writers, giving us an evening of eight plays. It was a huge success. The following year, we moved to a larger venue, expanded the run length, and made it an open competition. We received around 200 entries and sold out the entire run before opening night. *Diez Minutos* took place toward the end of March, when snowbirds, expats who come down from up north for the winter, were still here. I would never have attempted anything like this back in the U.S.; but here, in San Miguel, I found people to share the vision and help do

the work and appreciate the results. It turned out to be more than just a personal second act: it started a tradition. From *Diez Minutos*, I joined with other local playwrights to create the San Miguel Playwrights' Group, which still meets and produces its own annual Showcase.

My third "Second Act" in San Miguel is an act that came out of my association with the writers' conference. A part-time resident of San Miguel belonged to a Storytelling group in the Chicago area, where she lived full-time, and proposed starting an annual storytelling event in town. This seemed like the perfect location in many ways for celebrating the oral tradition. Unfortunately, there was no built-in infrastructure ready to assist. I became part of a team of five volunteers, and we agreed to help make it happen, working from the ground up with zero storytelling festival experience. At times the process was chaotic, forcing us to remain flexible, a key requirement for expat life in Mexico. We thought we had booked the auditorium at *Belles Artes*, a former convent and today considered by many to be one of the nicest art schools in the area, with its classic architecture, drop-dead gorgeous and serene landscaping, and located just a few blocks from the main plaza in *Centro*. The auditorium could seat 200, and we were pleased to have made the reservation. But about a month before our first performance date, we heard indirectly that *Belles Artes*, which is owned by the federal government, would be closed during the time of our festival for renovation. Nobody told us about the planned closure; our reservation had fallen through the cracks. Oy.

For a few days, we were distraught (but not surprised, mind you). Then, one of the volunteers rescued us by negotiating a sweetheart deal with *La Biblioteca*, San Miguel's bilingual public library, to rent their Santa Ana Theater, an intimate venue that seats only about 80, for an incredibly low price. Since our budget was based on a 200-seat space and we would be producing the festival in an 80-seat space, it was important that we found ways to make up the difference—and we did. The festival was mesmerizing, and still ranks as one of my favorite San Miguel experiences. I was only involved during the inaugural year of San Miguel's Storytelling Festival but it's still going on, and in 2019 celebrated its sixth year. The Showcase of Finalists became one of the most anticipated cultural events in town and is not only amazing but truly bilingual. If you have never been to or listened to a storytelling festival, I encourage you to try it out. Treat yourself to a few stories from "The Moth" available on YouTube to see what I mean. You'll get hooked.

Second acts may not be possible in America, according to the personal experience of Mr. Fitzgerald, but in San Miguel every expat can claim at least one second act. From finally learning to play Bridge to starting an NGO designed to help the local community, there are many opportunities to do something different with your life in this small mountain town in the middle of Mexico. Living here can be a game-changer, and if you move here, don't be afraid to reinvent yourself. Not many will judge and most will applaud. I know I've had more than my share of reinventions.

When I was a hiring manager, back in my working days, a person interviewing for a job quoted a scene from a movie, I recall it was a Star Trek movie, in which a main character said he only wanted to make a difference in life. Here you can—or not. It's totally up to you.

Well, that pretty much wraps up my ode to San Miguel. Will someone backstage please turn the audience prompter to "Applause." Hello? Anybody still there? Anybody? Beuller? Beuller?

They Died with their Fitbits On

In the wacky early Woody Allen movie *Sleeper*, the main character, health food store owner Miles Monroe, goes into the hospital for minor surgery. Something goes horribly wrong in theatre and, instead of walking out on his own a few hours later, he is cryogenically frozen, only to be thawed out like a packet of Bird's Eye peas 200 years later. A doctor tells Miles everyone he ever knew has been dead for a very long time. Miles is shocked and can't believe all his friends had died because they all ate organic rice.

I imagine Jeanne-Louise Calment, a French woman, didn't think twice about eating organic rice. She died at the age of one-hundred twenty-two years, five months. I like to think that lady could have made it to one-hundred-twenty-five if she didn't smoke. Yep, she smoked like a chimney almost to the end. Jeanne-Louise quit puffing only when she couldn't see to light her own cigarettes. Although she didn't own a Peloton bike, she took up fencing when she was still a spring chicken at the age of eighty-seven.

Some scientists claim under the right conditions a human can live a thousand years. That seems too ambitious.

Besides, can you imagine how many clothes you would need or how large your family Thanksgiving dinners would become? The human body is a machine and like any well-cared for machine it can run a very long time. Take a BMW, for example. It's not unusual to get three to four-hundred thousand miles on the same engine. Why? Because it's made to last and people who drive BMWs take good care of their car. Unless, of course, there's an accident on the road—or what I like to call "a sucker punch."

In a famous *New Yorker* cartoon by George Booth, a dispirited looking man stands on a street corner, on his way to or from work. He's wearing a hat, tie, overcoat, slacks, and dress shoes. He is unaware that out of the sky behind him an enormous divine hand is about to flick his hat into the street. He is about to get sucker punched.

Life is full of such examples. Chrysippus, an ancient Greek Stoic philosopher, gave his donkey wine, and then watched the drunken animal try to eat figs. The stoic laughed so hard he died and the donkey got the last bray; I believe it was the only time in history when a stoic died by epicurean means. The dancer Isadora Duncan was riding in a convertible, happy as a lark, until the wind blew her scarf into her face, strangling her to death. The philosopher and the dancer got sucker punched or, ahem, flicked. They didn't see it coming. The list of those who have been sucker punched into the bottomless pit is long and disturbing: a woman was killed by a falling Fast-Food sign; a man fatally struck down by fatigue after playing a video game for fifty hours. An entire soccer team wiped out by lightening during a game. The other team survived. Hmm. Perhaps the fix was in.

It seems there are more than a thousand ways to sucker punch a mortal. What's a human to do? Perhaps, the best we can hope for is to try and keep a few steps ahead of the Grim Reaper, whatever it takes. And that's why when our Medicare Advantage program provider offered to send us free Fitbits, we jumped at the chance and said to send those wrist bands our way.

Our free Fitbit was as basic as they come. The device was fully equipped with the capability to count steps and tell time. That's about it. I'm surprised we didn't have to manually wind it up every night. According to our program provider, we could purchase a more expensive device, one that tracked blood oxygen estimates, supported Alexa and Spotify, and gave us sleep stages and insights, including how much time spent in each sleep phase. When it comes to sleep, I'm binary: I'm either asleep or awake. If I wore something on my wrist that could tell me how much time I was asleep, I would never sleep. I'd be constantly looking at it to see how much sleep I was not getting. I'm the kind of guy who if someone complains about my snoring, I'll stay awake the next night to see if I actually do snore. If you think that's preposterous, you don't know me well.

Arlene and I are not just walkers, we're city walkers. In fact, during this, our third move to San Miguel, we are without a car. The last time we lived in the U.S., we felt we had spent far too much time riding in cars. However, this time in

Mexico, we both agreed, we're going to walk till we drop, a feat that actually happened in Paris many years ago.

We had been training to walk the Portland Marathon, the full 26 miles and whatever, so we felt our legs and lungs were up to any task. We attended a family wedding in New York that summer and decided to cross the pond to briefly visit both London and Paris. It was our first visit to either city but with only two and a half days to see Paris, we were not holding back. We even bought first-class tickets on Eurostar, the high-speed rail service connecting London to Paris. Our tickets included breakfast and a newspaper. As a cartoonist, I was professionally and morally obligated to choose "Bubble and Squeak" from the menu. Over the loud speaker, a conductor announced "Ninety seconds to the Chunnel"; excited, I put down the newspaper, pushed my breakfast aside, took another sip of coffee, and waited. Suddenly, the cabin turned dark and the lights went on. After several seconds of staring out into the darkness, I told Arlene, "Well, that's disappointing." She fired back: "What did you expect to see...Fish?" Perhaps I thought I'd see Bubble and Squeak. Instead, I saw dark walls. Bored with the change in scenery, I returned to reading the paper.

The second day, we tried to catch as much of the City of Lights as we could. It was as if we trying to mimic a ten-countries-in-six-days tour, only on foot and in less than a full day. Later that evening, we found ourselves far up the *Avenue des Champs-Élysées*, near the *Arc de Triomphe* and finally out of steam. No mas, no gas, no mas gas. That's when I took charge. Without a smartphone or a map, I decided to lead us out of the city lights and into the dark wilderness by carving a path that would save us many steps and bring us safely to our hotel in record time. I got this, I told Arlene.

Unfortunately, my short-cut was based on a geometrically consistent, logical urban design, involving parallel streets and intersecting ones that would lead us back to our hotel. In spite of Baron Haussmann's noble efforts, many of the streets in Paris, as we learned that night, were still medieval, chopped up, disorganized, charming but confusing, some seemingly circular in design. My short cut added at least an hour to the trek. By the time we made it back to our boutique hotel, somewhere between the Opera House and The Madeline, we were exhausted, too tired to even argue. We each took three Motrin tablets and collapsed on the bed, our legs shaking like Houghtaling's famous Magic Fingers Vibrating Bed.

Walking in San Miguel reminds me of walking the side streets of Europe, only without getting lost. The streets are often narrow and picturesque; the roadway covered in cobblestones. Raised sidewalks help keep pedestrians out of harm's way, and there are plenty of shops and cafes. Indeed, the bakeries here are some of the finest we've ever known, with almond croissants worthy of a Parisian *pâtisserie*. In the neighborhoods bordering *Centro*, a typical San Miguel house can be as colorful as a Calder painting or as rustic-looking as Jack London's cabin.

Walking gives us a chance to check out San Miguel up close and personal. The doors, for instance, are often architectural gems not to be missed, showcasing ornate carvings, unique door knockers, and striking combinations of wood and metal. What may appear small by the size of the door hides a much larger scene inside, from specialty shops and art galleries to open-air restaurants in a garden setting.

Is it safe to walk in San Miguel? In a word, yes. But we never walk late at night or in certain neighborhoods and we always practice safe walks. These days, we wear masks, sometimes two. Unfortunately, Arlene's ears are too small to comfortably hold a double mask in place. My over-sized ears, on the other hand, could handle five masks at the same time. I could sublet space on my face; in short, I'm a walking mask rack. But it's not the number of masks one wears that is most annoying. It's wearing one at all. Every time I wear a mask my nose starts to run, and I know I'm not alone.

What about the presence of Covid-19? The seven streets leading into the historic center of town are guarded by what Arlene refers to as "bouncy houses." These inflatable gates spray sanitizer over your body as you enter or leave *Centro.* That's not all. Crews of men in white uniforms and face shields spray sanitizer fluids over the buildings and streets. And there's more. If you are caught not wearing a mask in *Centro*, a local official will offer you one. Refuse to wear it and you could go to jail. When you enter a business, they take your temperature, record it, take down your name and phone number, and give you a spritz or dollop of hand sanitizer.

As a result, we mask up before heading out each morning on our walk. Every day we pass the same cryptic scene: a bag of cubed ice sitting on three huge ice blocks, all melting in front of a closed tienda. A logical guess would claim the daily delivery is made before the store opens. A logical solution would be better coordination. But rather than reschedule the time of delivery, the ice stands alone and melts.

Getting our mail and returning home takes 4,000 steps; paying our cable bill in person and back takes 13,000 steps. On some future date, no doubt, we will be unable to walk those steps, either easily or at all. Until then, armed with Fitbits on our wrist, we continue our peripatetic lives in San Miguel, onward and upward we walk, slouching toward *Centro*.

The Big Bug Theory

I come by my fear and distrust of scorpions honestly. As a young, malleable student in Catholic school I was shown a movie featuring a boy in rural Mexico who was stung by a scorpion. The boy slipped into a coma and only recovered through his family's strong faith and a miraculous visit by a saint. I don't remember which saint but it might have been the grand dame of Mexican Catholicism herself, Our Lady of Guadalupe, or perhaps a lesser light, St. Benadryl, the patron saint of scorpion bites.

Nonetheless, the film worked. I've lived in constant fear of those stingers ever since. And, of course, you can take the kid out of Catholic school but you can't take the Catholic school out of the kid. So, whenever I see a scorpion my first inclination is to pray. Within six months of our return to San Miguel, I confronted a scorpion crawling up our kitchen wall, and I succumbed to my second inclination. I whacked the sucker into oblivion with my shoe. The trick, of course, is to remove your shoe first before hitting the scorpion. Stepping on them is not only considered bad form but it is also a good way to get yourself stung. Payback is a mother, as they say.

These are not hale-and-well-met types, who pat a fellow scorpion on the back and make a toast in its honor in front of a dining hall full of other tipsy arthropods. If you see one in your house, there's a good chance you've seen them all. True to form, since dispatching that first scorpion with a size-eight loafer and I have yet to come face-to-face a second one. The word must have gotten out; I was to be avoided at all costs.

Other insects rushed to fill the void. Sometimes I think we're running a B&B for lower order insects. Mosquitoes arrive in spring and stick around through summer and into fall, nipping at our necks and arms and legs like we're chopped liver. And to them, we are. We burn citronella candles and incense sticks. We try to keep covered. We use anti-mosquito bug spray, which has been about as useful as waving a red blanket in front of an angry bull. We run a powerful fan in our bedroom at night, hoping the force of the wind will keep them at bay. But mosquitoes, as we all know, are persistent little kamikaze pilots and whatever opening they can find, which is usually an exposed ear, they gladly take.

But even bad things must come to an end and the mosquitoes, having gorged themselves at our all-you-can-eat buffet for months, usually pack up their bags when the nights and mornings turn cold, take a few antacids, and either move on to a warmer destination or go into hiding. That's when fall begins to mature and the grasshoppers arrive ready to feast on our plants. Living in Mexico has given us so many opportunities to give back to the Food Chain, I don't know where to begin.

Okay, I'll try. One night, during the first time living here, we were visiting friends for a movie and a meal in a rural neighborhood outside of town. I was responsible for providing the movie. After watching the movie in the upstairs room at our friend's house, everyone moved downstairs to eat dessert. We stayed behind to rewind the tape (it was a VHS tape, sorry to admit). Watching us on the wall behind their TV set was the largest spider I've ever seen outside of a museum.

"Oh my God," Arlene said. "Look at the size of that spider."

"Jesus," I said, only slightly more subdued.

The spider had an enormous bulbous body, from which extended eight incredibly long legs; it looked like something out of *The War of the Worlds*. If the spider had a chrome abdomen instead of black one, it could have been for sale at Hubcap City.

"We're not staying for dessert. I want to go home now," said Arlene.

We quickly finished rewinding the tape, ran downstairs, apologized, told everyone we couldn't stay for dessert, got in our car, and drove back to town to our rental house, where spiders were a more respectable, civilized size and weren't trying to take over the world.

If you haven't already guessed, Arlene is not what one would call outdoorsy. A New Yorker by birth and attitude, she is, in fact, what the Jack Palance character Curly in the movie *City Slickers* referred to with a snarl as "city folk."

I took her camping once, shortly after we were married, and have never since tried to duplicate the experience. The camping trip didn't start well and it didn't end well and in between it didn't go well; instead, there was what scripture conveniently refers to as the weeping and gnashing of teeth.

This is not news to anyone who knows us.

What was big news, however, was when we sold our downtown condo in Portland, Oregon, disposed of just about everything else we owned, dropped out, and moved to the middle of Mexico. Especially since, to belabor the point, my wife is not the roughing it type and most people up north imagined our lives down south to be the very definition of roughing it. Will you be able to access the internet, more than one friend asked, with a horrified look? Never mind shopping at Trader Joe's.

As it turned out, nothing could be further from the truth. We barely roughed it the first time we lived here and even less so the second time; we still enjoy most of the same amenities that cushioned our cushy lives in Portland. And yet, although we are not roughing it, we do live high in the mountains, in a semi-arid town, in a somewhat rustic location that has more than its share of bugs. Or, as Arlene would say in disgust: "things with wings." She hates things with wings and is somewhat terrified of them all, regardless if a winged thing is packing venom or just floating aimlessly and harmlessly through life thinking of writing its next Ode to Pollen.

And yet—bear with me, I'm almost there—we spent a good part of our time in Mexico outside. We walked just

about everywhere. We had a delightful interior courtyard that was open to the sky; we would have our morning coffee or afternoon happy hour in the interior courtyard. In addition, the house had a pleasant back courtyard where we would sometimes have lunch or dinner. It was in that back courtyard where it happened.

To pause for a moment, the weather in San Miguel at that time of year, early October, is almost always darn-near perfect and it was darn-near perfect that day. By October, we were past the hot and dusty season, had just exited the rainy season and only recently entered what many here consider to be weather nirvana: brisk mornings, warm afternoons, blue skies, cool nights, no rain. Such weather working in our favor, we elected to have our *comida* in the back courtyard.

With our meal over, as if part of a planned cabaret show that followed, a small bird or bat flew right at us. I ducked to avoid it; Arlene screamed. At the last second, the winged thing veered off and flitted up the side of our house. That's when we got a good look at the UFO or, to use the more current term, UAP.

Neither bird nor bat, it was an enormous and magnificent Monarch butterfly and for a moment we were both speechless. We had seen moths and butterflies before, of course, but never one that size or quite that impressive. It strafed us one more time before flying over our high wall and out of sight, heading south as part of the annual Monarch butterfly migration from Canada to Mexico. I read someplace that the Monarch butterfly is the only butterfly to do an annual two-way migration the same as birds (and some expats), leaving their snow shovels in Toronto for a leafy sanctuary in the mountains of central Mexico.

We talked about the Monarch butterfly in awe for several minutes and Arlene admitted it was the kind of thing with wings she could learn to appreciate. It was a gorgeous, flying painting. We saw more butterflies, smaller ones, for weeks after, but nothing to equal the grandeur of the one that entertained us that day.

I thought back to when we were visiting a relative in South Florida many years earlier. On the way to their house from the airport, we passed several strip malls. One mall had a fast-food restaurant with an unusual name: Wings and Things. As we passed it, I noticed something even more unusual. Wings and Things was closed and totally covered in a tarp because they were spraying for termites. The sight of the big sign promoting "Wings and Things" next to a huge exterminator's tent was a delicious Kodak-moment. Unfortunately, I did not have a camera with me.

I also didn't have it with me when the giant Monarch butterfly visited us. But next time I will… because those wings were something. In the famous words from a Seinfeld episode: "They're real. And, they're spectacular."

Where Have All My Punchlines Gone?

I should have seen it coming. Thirty years ago, I was a marketing manager and leading a department meeting when the first sign unexpectedly reared its head. All my direct reports were under 30 years of age—I was not. During cross-talk, one of them said she had never been to Spain. Of course, not one to let an obvious opening close without comment, I piped up: "But I kind of like the music." All hail Three Dog Night.

My remark was met with confused stares and a long stretch of awkward silence. I was thinking they just didn't get it; they were thinking I was showing early signs of dementia.

And therein lies the rub: how does someone navigate in a world where nobody understands his or her reference points? What happens to a lifetime of handy pop cultural callbacks that no longer resonate? Let's face it, it's not as if you can easily drop a Judy Garland-Mickey Rooney or Sonny and Cher reference and replace it with Beyonce and Jay Z. Okay, maybe the Sonny and Cher swap would work. But that's an exception.

The truth is, all those wonderful and witty comebacks you've saved over a lifetime of making smart-ass comments are about as useful as Monopoly money in a Las Vegas casino. So, the next time you're with your grandchildren—or with anyone from a post-Boomer generation—try using Maxwell Smart's "He missed it by that much" or Sergeant Schultz' refrain of "I see Nothing. I know Nothing!" or Desi Arnaz' trademark "Lucy! I'm home!" and see where that gets you.

Sadly, when you have to start explaining your punchlines, it's time to settle on a sofa and turn on a game show. My maternal grandmother, for example, loved game shows. In her late 80s and living with an aunt, the two of them spent their evenings watching TV game shows. One such evening, according to my aunt, the question asked was embarrassingly simple; I suspect the show might have been Hollywood Squares. The emcee asked "Who's buried in Grant's Tomb?" My grandmother blurted out: "Cary Grant." It was an answer worthy of Paul Lynde.

What brought all this to mind was indeed a game show. I enjoy watching "Jeopardy!" but found a recent episode disturbing. More about that soon.

But first, my favorite moments in Jeopardy often occur after the first commercial break, when the late and great Alex Trebek would briefly interview each contestant about a piece of trivia in their life. He always maintained his composure, even when faced with mundane details that could make a roasted coffee bean slip into a coma. I never made

it on the show, mostly because I never applied or took the Jeopardy test. But, had I been on the show, I had my personal story ready to tell:

ALEX: "I understand, Mark, you once owned an unusual car."

ME: "Yes, Alex, that's true. I once owned a Yugo, the cheapest new car in America and still over-priced. In the movie 'Dragnet,' they referred to the Yugo as being on the cutting edge of Serbo-Croatian technology. When I bought the car, they gave me a t-shirt that said: 'Wherever I go, Yugo.' I got rid of the car a year later and kept the shirt."

Back to the disturbing Jeopardy episode. The three contestants, many years my junior, were shown an image of the star playing Mister Rogers in the movie "A Beautiful Day in the Neighborhood." They were asked to name the movie star.

Not one of the contestants answered. I was stunned. They didn't even buzz in to venture a guess. They stood there with blank expressions and empty tablets and watched as an equally stunned Alex told them the answer. But before he could, I jumped up and shouted at the screen: "Tom Hanks. You idiots, Tom Hanks. Tom Hanks. Tom Hanks!"

I collapsed on the sofa. Suddenly, I felt untethered and adrift. It was as if Francis the Talking Mule had quit talking to Mister Ed. Now try explaining that reference to a Gen Zer.

Go ahead, make my day.

How I Found Joy Before I Found the Internet

I know what you're thinking and it wasn't that. Get your mind out of the gutter. To steal a line from the western-comedy "Support Your Local Sheriff," puberty hit me hard but not that hard. Granted, the day after puberty arrived, I had to start wearing eyeglasses. Which is not as dramatic as my cartoonist friend Gary. In his mind, he believed he had invented erections and once considered entering his penis in the school science fair. Wiser minds prevailed.

I guess I was easily amused as a child. I suppose I still am. Born in 1949, I grew up the middle child in a middle-class family in Northern California, living in a series of cookie-cutter suburban communities. As a side note, my parents lived in more than forty different houses or apartments during the first fifty years of their marriage. For the longest time as a child, I thought "Escrow" was the name of some old geezer who was hoarding my parents' money and refusing to release the funds.

My sister, two years older, was always outgoing and exceedingly popular no matter where we landed. I went the

other direction. Whenever adults described me, they always inserted a modifier: they said I was terribly shy or horribly shy or, the most painful of all, painfully shy. If "Most Likely to be Marked Absent by Mistake" had been a school contest category, I would have won it hands down. Then again, nobody would be able to remember my name.

Being shy was okay because I surrounded myself with words and pictures. Compensating for a lack of nearby book stores, I visited the library often and earned an early reputation for racking up overdue fees. It's a habit I couldn't break even as an adult and a shame I shall carry to my grave.

At home, I owned volumes of Hardy Boys books, while an aunt would let me borrow volumes from her collection of Oz books. I was an early mash-up artist and, in my imagination, would think of unwritten books waiting to be published, including such destined to be best-sellers such as The Hardy Boys in the Mystery of the Missing Tik-Tok in the Land of Oz or The Hardy Boys and the Sinister Captain Salt of Oz. Now that I think about it, some books are better left unwritten.

Of course, I inhaled comic books and had amassed the kind of collection that if owned today could easily cover my 401k losses from 2007.

I also loved reading the newspaper comics page, especially the Sunday edition and its colorful, over-sized drawings. Thanks to an ingenious product known as Silly Putty, I could spend an entire afternoon with the Sunday comics (I told you I was easily amused). I would take the putty, slap it on a favorite comic strip, press hard, and pull away, capturing an image of the strip. And that's when the fun really started, because by stretching the putty I could distort the image. By the time I was done with stout and bearded Bluto, he was as thin as an Abba-Zaba bar at a taffy-pulling contest.

My favorite indoor pastime, however, was a word game a friend and I played, long before "Words with Friends" became a popular smartphone app. We would comb through a dictionary for a long word, find one, and write it at the top of a sheet of paper. Next, writing furiously and separately for thirty minutes, we would compose as many words as we could think of, using only the letters at the top of the page.

"Antidisestablishmentarianism," clocking in at a long 28 letters, was our favorite starter word. We were told it was the longest word in the English language and had no reason to doubt it. As an asthmatic, I could barely pronounce the word without taking big gulps or wheezing after the fifth syllable.

One day my partner-in-words brought in a medical dictionary and that single change lifted our game to an entirely new level:

Pneumonoultramicroscopicsilicovolcanoconiosis

Today, I usually start my morning by playing the Spelling Bee game in the *New York Times*. The game is simple. You try to make as many words as you can out of seven letters that appear in a circle or "wheel." Each word must be a least four letters long and must include the letter in the center of the wheel.

Which brings me to a different point: what is the purpose of a silent letter? Isn't it about time the other letters, you know, the ones actually doing all the work, slap silent letters with a class action lawsuit? Silent letters do nothing and still get paid. How fair is that? Wait a minute. On second thought, if we fire all the silent letters in the English language, then Shakespeare would be a "riter" instead of a writer. Silent letters get to stay. No harm, no foul. But, aha, what about those people who cause language inflation by adding "a lot" to whatever they say? A plain thanks is no longer good enough. These days it has to be "thanks a lot."

Those early years were influential yet, oddly enough, I didn't grow up to become a sales rep for Big Pharma or a medical librarian. Although, I did work in a medical library while in college, a questionable job for a hypochondriac. From working as a journalist in the United States Navy to teaching English composition at a small university, from magazine cartooning and screenwriting to crafting user manuals and marketing materials in high tech, I remained loyal to my roots. I was a "word and picture" kind of guy. Still am. You can take my word on it. Or I can sketch an artist's rendering, not to scale.

If Music be the Food of Insomnia

Where have you gone, Sheb Wooley? I suppose every generation venerates the music of its youth. As a Boomer, I am particularly grateful for the music I grew up with. We had folk songs and surfer music, Country and Motown, not to mention the British Invasion; gentle pop tunes from the 50s eventually gave way to more radical songs of the 60s. An embarrassment of riches for growing minds.

Long before my generation fell in love with the poetic songs and wretched voice of Bob Dylan, we were fed a steady diet of inane lyrics: "The Purple People Eater," "Itsy Bitsy Teenie Weenie Yellow Polka Dot Bikini," and just about anything by Allan Sherman. I'm sure younger generations have their own music legends but, let's face it, Lady Gaga is no Sam the Sham and the Pharaohs.

And therein lies my problem. I have what's known as an earworm. Fortunately—or unfortunately—I am not alone. Something like ninety percent of us suffer through the pangs and arrows of an earworm on a regular basis.

In case you fall into the ten percent group and are unfamiliar with the concept of an earworm, it's simple: an

earworm is a song that gets stuck in your head. Sounds harmless enough, until it happens to you, especially when you're trying to sleep and can't because your mind plays that stupid song in a loop, over and over and over, and you have an important presentation to make at work later that same day and know you're going to feel crappy during the presentation and will most likely blow it.

Researchers, of course, can explain an earworm. They even have other names for it: cognitive itch, sticky music, stuck-song syndrome. Most often, the culprit is a song you recently heard. It might replay itself because you're under stress. Or, as one theory holds, it's directly tied to the human oral storytelling tradition, where memorization was critical to survival.

I'm sharing this information with you because a couple of evenings ago I was streaming Amazon Music in the comfort of my home. I wanted something upbeat and uncomplicated, so I chose an album of the top 100 songs from the 1950-60s. That was my first mistake.

My second mistake was listening to "The Witch Doctor" by David Seville. I first became familiar with that song when I was almost ten, in 1958, sixty years ago and change. I don't recall hearing it often, if at all, since. Now if I had my wits about me and better reflexes, I would have raced over, grabbed the remote and put it on mute before the song started. But I didn't, and I paid the price. All night long, unable to reach inside my head and turn my brain off, all I could hear was: "Ooo eee, ooo ah ah ting tang / Walla walla, bing bang."

I guess it could have turned out worse. Seville also gave us "The Chipmunk Song."

Free Rubber Chickens

As something of a self-proclaimed word and picture guy, I looked forward one night to seeing the 2013 rom-com *Words and Pictures*, starring Juliette Binoche and Clive Owen. In the movie, she's a talented abstract painter, who teaches art to high school students, and he's a talented writer, who teaches English to students at the same school. There's a wager made between the two battling love interests over which is most powerful: words or pictures?

But what I thought would be a paean to creativity turned out in its sub-plot to be an endorsement of censorship. I was disappointed that they chose to pick on a young male cartoonist for his clumsy but sexist caricature of a fellow student, a girl he had a crush on. The school administrators punished the boy for his crude drawing. In my opinion, they could have found a better subplot, one that didn't decapitate creativity with a censor's axe.

I suppose I might have been overly sensitive about the issue that evening, because earlier in the day I had read a news story about the Iranian female political cartoonist Atena Farghadani. She had been sentenced to 12 years in prison for drawing a cartoon that showed members of the Iranian parliament with the heads of cows and monkeys. In many ways, it was a drawing reminiscent of a classic Thomas Nast cartoon; politicians shown as animals is a well-trodden path in the realm of editorial cartooning. The Iranian supreme leader was not amused.

Algeria was not amused with cartoonist Tahar Djehiche, who was arrested, tried, and sent to jail for insulting President Bouteflika. Nor was Turkey, who arrested newspaper cartoonist Musa Kart and sentenced him to jail time. Venezuelan newspaper cartoonist Rayma Suprani was fired over her cartoons about the government and currently lives in exile in the United States. Tunisian blogger Jabeur Mejri was sentenced to seven and a half years in prison in 2012 for reposting cartoons on Facebook. The beat goes on.

In Paris on January 7, 2015, two men forced their way inside the offices of Charlie Hedbo, a French weekly satirical newspaper, and killed 12 people while injuring 11 others. The men were angered by cartoon depictions of the Prophet Muhammad. *Je suis Charlie.*

So much anger over quick sketches that use dots for eyes.

When I'm depressed at how this "lowly" artform is treated, for solace I turn to my favorite quote from cartoonist B. Kliban: "But the technologists have got their toys and they're going to play with them. Like, if cartoonists had all that money, we sure as hell would use it. There would be weird cartoon sculptures five-hundred feet high, and free rubber chickens, regardless of a person's religious belief."

The word "cartoon" comes from the Italian "cartone" and Dutch word "karton." It entered the language toward the end of the Italian Renaissance and means strong, heavy paper or pasteboard used to make a full-size drawing as a study for a work of art. One of the early popular uses of these cartoons was in the production of frescoes, in which the image would include pinpricks to outline its design. But I've noticed seeds or aspects of the cartooning craft throughout history, starting with the earliest cave paintings. Please join me as I stroll through a diorama of cartooning through the ages, making anachronistic associations along the way.

We start at a prehistoric cave in France, *Pech Merle*, a cave that's covered with painted murals created between 25,000 years and 16,000 years BC. Wooly mammoths, horses, bulls, reindeer, and, most especially, human handprints cover the cave's walls. The images look like Japanese ink paintings in their Zen-like simplicity and fluidity. But to me, what's most memorable are the many handprints next to the paintings. It's as if the creator said: "I made this. I was here."

Our next stop is ancient Egypt to observe hieroglyphics, a mix of symbols, pictograms, and alphabetic elements that became one of the earliest forms of written language. The iconic, cartoon-like images of hieroglyphics, an ancient form of emoji, if you will, preserve and tell a story. If you've seen one glyph, you've seen 'em all, so we'll fast forward to the 11th century and take a close look at the Bayeaux Tapestry, the leading graphic novel of its time, that rolls out like an endless hall carpet, 70-feet long and 20 inches wide. During one vacation, I saw the tapestry in person, which, as the internet reminds us, is not a real tapestry because the design is embroidered and not woven. Okay, whatever. But when seeing the Bayeaux Tapestry up-close and personal, it is hard to ignore the prescient comic art style of storytelling exhibited on that cloth.

We arrive several centuries later to stare slack-jawed in wonder at Master Hieronymus Bosch's most famous painting "The Garden of Earthly Delights." I don't know about you, but my eyes are wide-open, taking in the many images, while drool forms at the corner of my mouth. It's a surreal picture that could easily be a mashup of the best of Salvador Dali and cartoonist Gahan Wilson. My first reaction is to tell the waiter I'll have what he's having. Then, quickly I change my mind, as we sprint forward and roll into the 20th century. And this is where I choose to stop my tour for a moment and sigh. Deeply. Sadly. I am heart-broken.

One word: *Guernica*. The mural "*Guernica*" by Pablo Picasso is the greatest anti-war political cartoon in history, in my opinion. The painting, in stark black and white and gray paint, depicts the horrific bombing of the town of *Guernica*, Spain, an ancient and defenseless Basque town, by German and Italian warplanes on April 26, 1937. The bombing raids occurred because Hitler wanted to test Germany's war machine, anticipating a much larger engagement on the horizon. At the time, the town was mostly inhabited by women and children. The bombing continued for over two hours, with fighter planes using their machine guns to strafe

people hiding in the fields to finish them off. It was a massacre. There is a story about how Picasso while living in Nazi-occupied Paris during World War II was being harassed by a Gestapo officer. The officer pointed to a photo of the painting *Guernica* and asked, "Did you do that?" Picasso, according to the story, said, "No, you did."

After moments of somber reflection, we fast forward again, but this time to the Age of Aquarius. In the 1960s, Dan O'Neill, creator of the comic strip "Odd Bodkins" and other cartoons, became a legend in cartoon circles. O'Neill founded the Air Pirates, a group of underground comics that drew parodies of Disney characters. Disney was not amused and sued. After the other Air Pirates members had settled with Disney, O'Neill continued, dragging the case on for years. He eventually lost and was ordered to pay something in the neighborhood of $200,000. At the time, he probably had less than $100 in his bank account, owned no appreciable assets, and drove a crappy car. Disney and O'Neill agreed finally to a settlement, case closed. One day during the case, however, O'Neill showed up at the federal building in San Francisco dressed as a villain from a Western: black everywhere, cowboy hat, boots, a holster with a banana stuck inside. As he exited the elevator, an armed guard ran toward him and slammed him against a wall, screaming: "He's got a banana!" Although O'Neill lost the case, he always contended he had won. "Doing something stupid once is just plain stupid," said O'Neill. "Doing something stupid twice is a philosophy."

With the tour over, you are now free to move around the cabin. And that's my cartoonist tribe for you, pointing out human folly and idiocy, poking their finger in the eye of the Evil Eye, even for a lost cause, and I'm proud to be a member of it. But these editorial and underground cartoonists represent the courageous family branch. I come from a different branch, one known not for its provocative stands in speaking truth to power but for its sense of whimsy in tickling funny bones. If editorial cartoonists are the knights in shining armor, I'm from the court jester branch, what's known as a gag cartoonist.

A gag is a funny idea; a gag cartoon is a funny idea that's been illustrated. Gag cartoonists make connections most people don't make, but those same people will react to the cartoon by smiling or laughing. Gag cartoons appear in magazines and newspapers. Getting published in *The New Yorker*, for example, is considered the high-water mark in the career of any gag cartoonist. There is a story told about the early days at *The New Yorker*. E.B. White and James Thurber, as staff writers, shared an office. Thurber would occasionally sketch a cartoon and throw it away. White would retrieve the discarded cartoon. Eventually, the magazine began publishing Thurber's cartoons, drawn in a primitive style a fellow writer described as resembling half-baked cookie dough. One day, a more accomplished illustrator complained to Harold Ross, the editor, that they were no longer using his cartoons but, instead, were publishing cartoons by "that fifth-rate cartoonist Thurber." Ross, according to the story,

rose to Thurber's defense and said Thurber was not fifth-rate, he was third-rate.

In the same way I can always remember a good meal, I never forget a good gag. To illustrate what I mean by a gag, here are three examples by other gag cartoonists, that still rank high in my memory.

Example 1: It's an executive's office. Across from the executive sits a job seeker. The executive is placing the phone back. The caption? "Your references asked me to hold you here until the police arrive."

Example 2: We see the back of a conductor leading an orchestra. On his music stand, in large print are the words: "Wave the stick in the air until the music stops, then turn and bow."

Example 3: An anthropomorphic version of a hot dog, complete with eyes, legs, and arms, is stranded on a small island in the ocean. He's reading from a message in a bottle that's washed ashore. The caption reads: "Congratulations, you may already be a wiener."

I admit that last gag is a real groaner, but I still love it. Gag cartoonists will often take a common or trite setup—in this case, it was the stranded on an island trope—and play with it. They see everyday things differently. For example, when I lived in Oregon, I would drive by a cemetery on my way home. A huge sign on the cemetery grounds promoted "Full Cremation Services."

To a cartoonist, this means that if they have a full-service, they must also offer a partial-service. So, what's that like? "We crisp him up to the torso and you take care of the rest."

Gags don't have to be within a single frame. One of my favorite Jules Feiffer cartoons is a multi-panel drawing that shows a woman outside her sick husband's hospital room. She's clearly nervous and distraught, smoking and pleading with God. She tells God that her husband is a good man and if God would spare his life, she'll become a good person, too. She'll treat people better, start attending church, and so on. She takes a puff of her cigarette, thinks for a second. Then tells God, "If you have to take anyone … take the doctor."

Sometimes a gag is more character-driven. The incomparable comic strip "Pogo" by Walt Kelly, for example, took its gags and stories from the Okefenokee Swamp characters he created. In one panel, Pogo Possum has narrowly escaped the clutches of some very bad characters who were planning to boil and eat him. Pogo recovers in a hospital bed and is visited by Porky Pine, a gloomy character of very few words. But, he's there to cheer up Pogo and show his friend his support. Porky Pine sits next to Pogo and doesn't say anything for a few frames. Pogo watches him closely. Finally, Porky Pine looks over at Pogo and says, "I want you to know that had they cooked ya, I wouldn't have et any of you."

Gag cartoons are known as magazine filler, and that's pretty much how I started cartooning. As part of a team of Navy journalists assigned to the United States Seabees, we were required to create and publish a monthly magazine whenever we were on an overseas deployment. To fill up copy

space, I started drawing cartoons. A lifelong doodler, I took to cartooning like a tape worm at an all-you-can-eat buffet. This was before they had books teaching you how and where to send gag cartoons. Fortunately, *Writer's Digest Magazine* published a weekly column on cartooning and that's where I received my first lessons.

The submission process was simple. Usually, a cartoonist would draw a batch of gags, five to ten, and send them to an appropriate magazine. The magazine would buy or hold what they liked and reject the rest; the latter happened a lot more often than the former.

I sent my first batch of seven cartoons to *Playboy Magazine*. They were, of course, all rejected, but it was the best rejection a newbie cartoonist could hope for: a real letter, signed by the cartoon editor, and carrying the embossed seal of the magazine. Undeterred, I sent the same batch to a new magazine looking for "Playboy-style" cartoons and they bought three. I was on clouds nine through fifteen. Unfortunately, the only person who could find the magazine with my cartoons in it was my grandfather, a retired Western Pacific railroad man. He located the magazine in a cigar store in Oakland, California, stashed among other tacky adult magazines. My grandfather cut my silly cartoons—there was nothing prurient about them—from the magazine and placed them in the family Bible. On one side of each tear sheet was my cartoon, on the other was lurid text along the lines of "She grabbed his throbbing missile, ready for lift-off."

At first, I drew cartoons with a classic dip pen, a Crow Quill as I recall. After that I started using a basic black marker pen, sometimes an extra fine Sharpie. Later, I used a software program called SuperPaint on a Macintosh computer. The program combined bitmap painting and vector drawing. When *The Saturday Evening Post* bought one of my cartoons, they asked for the original. I told them I had created the cartoon on my computer and I wasn't sending them my Macintosh. The editor wrote back to tell me they had a policy of not accepting "computer generated art" but didn't think my drawing looked as if it came from a computer. They paid me and ran the cartoon. No magic involved. These days, I'm back to drawing with a marker pen, whenever I draw. Tools are merely tools.

While working in the Silicon Valley during the early Eighties, I joined a San Francisco Bay area group of cartoonists and writers. A few members were shining stars of the cartoon universe, such as Charles Schulz ("Peanuts"), Hank Ketcham ("Dennis the Menace"), and Gus Arriola ("Gordo"). Most members, however, were like me: no name cartoonist wannabes who had been drawing since they were in diapers. Our monthly meetings usually featured a guest cartoonist, such as Garry Trudeau ("Donnesbury") or Sergio Aragonés (*MAD Magazine*, *Groo the Wanderer*). The featured cartoonist would give a "chalk talk" and draw a few cartoons while delivering a presentation. After the talk, the guest would answer questions. A fellow member would always ask the same question: "What kind of pen do you use?"

I imagine he thought there was magic in a specific pen and if he could find the right bibbidi-bobbidi-boo pen, his cartooning career would be set. If only that were true.

After Arlene and I moved to Portland, Oregon, I missed getting together with fellow cartoonists. As a result, I joined forces with two other local cartoonists and started what eventually became COW (Cartoonists of the Willamette). To bring together enough cartoonists to form a group, we held a cartoon art contest at a pizza parlor in downtown Portland on a Saturday.

We had no idea if anyone would show up. When the three of us arrived at the pizza parlor a half-hour before the contest began, we were stunned to see a long line of people with sketch pads and portfolios waiting. The price to enter a cartoon was only ten dollars; the prizes were nothing more than drawing pads, colored pencils, marker pen sets, and the like. Nothing to write or draw home about, and no cash whatsoever. A few minutes before the closing of our entry window, a man rushed up with a drawing and asked if he still had time to enter. He told me he had already entered one drawing and just sold blood to pay for a second entry fee. His cartoon was unimpressive and didn't have a chance of winning. I wanted to urge him to get his blood back. But that wasn't his point. Like the image of a hand painted on a prehistoric cave wall, it was enough for him to say, "I was here. I made this."

The charming, idyllic small town of Silverton, Oregon, gateway to Silver Falls Park with its ten waterfalls, holds an annual three-day festival over the first weekend in August in honor of a cartoonist, a local boy named Homer Davenport, who became one of the highest paid and most respected political cartoonists in the world in the 1890s. He was also one of the first American breeders of Arabian horses. The annual festival boasts a variety of events, from a parade to an arts and crafts fair, from an Arabian horse show to an international cartoon art contest—and, last but not least, their signature Davenport Race. Someone on the festival committee heard about COW and invited us to attend, encouraging our members to enter the cartoon art contest. They asked if we wanted to participate in the couch race. We jumped at the chance.

We didn't know the first thing about preparing for a couch race but were told it was nothing more than a sofa on wheels that you push down a street. Easy peasy-pillow squeezy. We affixed a dumpy sofa on top of an old Red Wagon Flyer and, after practice runs down a friend's street, we were pleased with our contraption. The ends of the sofa wobbled like the ends of a pole a high-wire artist carries for balance. Still, mission accomplished. We christened it "Couch Potato," and decorated it with a cardboard TV set, a fake remote, and a few empty bags of fast-food detritus. A COW member wore his Viking hat with dual horns and Betty Boop underwear over pajama bottoms. He stood tall and proud in the middle of the sofa as if he were General Patton leading his tanks into battle. Couch Potato was a big hit during the morning parade. Shortly after noon it all fell apart.

We showed up at the race starting point and were assigned a heat. We'd be racing against two other sofa teams. Certainly, we expected competition. What we didn't expect was to compete against professionals. The other sofas all looked as if they could race at the NASCAR level. Their "davenports" were sponsored by local taverns, restaurants, and stores, and fielded by what could easily pass for NIKE-branded athletes under contract, both men and women, in matching outfits. Our contraption was barely worth competing in a soap box derby. It will come as no surprise, I'm sure, to learn the wheels came off of our wagon half-way down the street during our one and only heat. After much confusion resembling a silent film comedy, where we ran around the sofa bumping into each other, we grabbed Couch Potato, lifted it and carried the tacky home furnishing across the finish line, dead last and by a long shot. All was not lost, however. We won a participation trophy.

And that, ladies and gentlemen, encapsulates why I love cartoonists.

At my mother's funeral, an old friend of hers, a former teacher, asked me if I were still drawing. I told her rarely these days, and only upon request. She told me she loved how as a kid I was always drawing, and how she thought my sketches showed promise. She said I may not have known this but the nuns at my school were appalled that I was always doodling in my notebooks. They called my mother in for a parent-teacher conference to discuss my constant drawing; idle hands, the devil's workshop, get thee behind me, and all that nonsense. They were afraid I was not paying sufficient attention in class and asked my mother to talk to me about it and get me to change my ways. They were sincerely worried for my soul. After meeting with the nuns, my mother sought advice from her teacher friend, who told my mother the nuns were flat-out nuts. As a teacher, you want to encourage creativity, not stifle it, she told my mom. I had no clue the nuns had me in their sight. My mother kept the meeting to herself and never mentioned a word of it to me.

In thinking back, I believe that was the Christmas my parents bought me a Jon Gnagy "Learn to Draw" kit, and the following Christmas I received my first set of oil paints.

Onward and Upward, Sideways and Sideways

After living in San Miguel for the second time—for a period of five years—we decided to pull up stakes and return to Oregon. This time, instead of returning to Portland, we were moving to the town of Medford in the beautiful Rogue Valley at the southern end of the state. For reasons we are still unable to digest, we decided to leave the wonderful, delightful, friendly, lively, artsy, beautiful, cosmopolitan, charming, colonial, [enter your choice of modifier here] town of San Miguel de Allende in the central highlands of Mexico and move back to the United States. After we left, San Miguel was chosen by *Travel+Leisure* readers as their favorite city in the world for two years in a row. Coincidence or fate? You make the call. More recently, 715,000 *Condé Nast Traveler* readers voted for their favorite travel experiences around the world and picked San Miguel as The Best Small City in the World, ahead of such cities as Florence, Monte Carlo, and Chiang Mai, to name but three other cities in the top ten list. Earlier, back in 2008, the historic center of San Miguel had been designated a UNESCO World Heritage Site.

What. Were. We. Thinking?

Unable to find a decent rental that would accept an 85-pound dog, a psychotic cat with sharp claws, and two aging retirees, we decided to buy a small house in southern Oregon. Only one of us could fly to the United States ahead of time and find our new place. Arlene elected to stay with our pets in San Miguel, where she would continue working on the logistics of moving us from one country to another.

Meanwhile, I flew to California, rented a car, and drove north to seek our next home. Friends thought Arlene was insane to send me alone to find us a house in Oregon. To them, it was as if George Custer had hired Soupy Sales to find a good camping spot along the Little Big Horn. But this is the 21st century, not 1876, and we did plenty of research over the internet before I left. I carried with me a list of nine houses to check out in person in a single afternoon. I needed to act fast, especially since a moving company was already scheduled to pick up our things and take them to Oregon. We wanted to tell them where to deliver the goods, otherwise they could find themselves a land-based version of *The Flying Dutchman*.

In my defense, it's not as if I didn't have any house-hunting experience. The first house we bought in Portland was as good as any place to start the learning process. Unfortunately, the hot water heater blew up three weeks after we moved in. During the repair work, we discovered that nothing was in-code, and we were lucky the house was still standing. The previous owner was a do-it-yourselfer type who didn't know

what he was doing. On the advice of our real estate agent, we chose not to do an inspection. First lesson learned. Always get a home inspection before purchase. And find a better real estate agent.

Our second purchase was a local builder's spec house. We traded our equity for a down payment and gladly moved in. The house was new and had an impressive view of Mt. Hood, with 180-degrees of tall windows. But the slap-dash finish work was largely unfinished. Every closet rod in the house fell down within weeks, as if the closets had a built-in self-destruct timer. The house was half-way up a steep driveway; whenever it snowed, our driveway seemed to be the last in the metro region to thaw. We referred to it as the Huber Street Glacier. The first time I pulled the car out of the garage after a snow storm I took down part of a neighbor's fence. From that point on, as a precaution, whenever it snowed, we would park our car on the street below. Arlene would walk gingerly down the steep driveway to the car. On the other hand, I'd walk as if there were no snow on the ground whatsoever. One morning, I slipped on the icy surface, fell on my back, and slid all the way down to the bottom, doing my impersonation of a luge run in the Winter Olympics, stopping only because my moving body collided with the unmovable base of a sturdy tree. I could hear Arlene laughing as I whizzed by.

We found living in a new house much to our liking, so we chose to build our next house. Unfortunately, the house was in a suburban community and far away from any action.

During the work week, by the time both of us had made it through rush hour traffic from our respective jobs to our new house, we were too tired to go out again. And then it happened. Arlene was having dinner one evening with a friend at a small Italian restaurant in The Pearl, a popular urban Portland neighborhood. I was home with the pets, eating leftovers and watching reruns on television. Conversation at home was limited. Arlene called, and I could hear all the excitement going on in the background: music, laughter, chatter, the happy opposite of the sounds of silence. The restaurant had blocked off part of a street so everyone could play bocce ball. After that experience (or, in my case, missed experience), we decided to sell our suburban house and move into the city.

Our next house purchase was a condo in the King's Hill neighborhood just below the entrance to Washington Park. It was love at first sight. We had one of those so-called million-dollar views enjoyed by non-millionaires of downtown Portland and the Columbia River, as well as of Mt. Hood and Mt. Adams. It was a seventh-floor corner unit, with two bedrooms and two bathrooms, facing East. After we had been in our new condo for about a month, one of our neighbors visited. She sat with Arlene and talked about the building's history and some of the people in it. At one point in the conversation, this person said she loved our unit and had thought about buying it herself, even though she already lived in the building. She mentioned the condo had stayed on the market a long time because of its history. I immediately interjected

myself into their conversation. What history, I asked? Our neighbor was surprised we didn't know the previous owner had been murdered in our condo unit.

She filled us in on the story. The deceased former owner was an older man who worked with at-risk kids and had a fondness for young street women. He took the wrong one home to his condo one night. Things got out of hand and the woman cracked him over the head with a bottle of jug wine. She finished him off Lizzie Borden-style by whacking him several times with a cast-iron skillet. Post-murder, she took his wallet, car keys, and car, leaving the dead body in her wake on what was now our kitchen floor. Both Arlene and I had remembered the murder; it was a big local news story for several days.

Three years after moving into the condo, we were moving again. This time we were dropping out and moving to the middle of Mexico, where we didn't know a soul and could barely speak the language. Our two very different computer industry jobs with two very different companies were both going away, coincidently around the same time. We couldn't afford to keep the condo unless we worked, but we were too old for the computer business to secure new jobs, even though we had lived in the area for over twenty years and had plenty of local contacts. We thought about trying to cobble together part-time jobs until the economy turned around. But we lacked the energy or enthusiasm; we were flat-out tired of the high-tech grind. That's when we discovered and ended up in San Miguel de Allende.

The first house I checked out in Medford was at the top of our modest budget and was dreadful—inside and out. I didn't even bother to call Arlene. The second house was not much better. The third could have doubled as a laboratory, where for the last twenty years they had stress-tested cigarette smokers. It was a giant ashtray with walls, shrouded in a constant haze. I wasn't sure we'd ever get the smoke out of the house or our lungs. The fourth house I looked at was getting closer to our wish list but a wall in the back of the house was ominous. It looked like the infamous garage wall in Chicago where Al Capone's gang shot and killed seven members of a rival gang on Valentine's Day in 1929. Something resembling blood splatters were everywhere.

Eventually, I narrowed our selection to two houses: an adorable 1920s white house with a white picket fence and a 1990s updated house in a great neighborhood with a small fenced yard and a detached garage. Our real estate agent gave me a copy of the home inspection report for the 1920s house. With a previous disagreeable out-of-code experience, we didn't want to take the risk on a house that was going to immediately require work. We sought turn-key, not fixer-upper. The home inspection report read like *The Shining*. So, we bought the 1990s house, and I returned to San Miguel to help pack and move.

We left San Miguel early in the morning in April. A moving company had already picked up our belongings, leaving us with a packed car, a screaming cat in a pet carrier, and a large dog, who had to sit high on his bed, hunched over

like Andre the Giant entering the home of Bilbo Baggins. The one-day drive to Laredo normally would take about ten hours, and I definitely did not want to drive in Mexico after dark. I made sure we allowed plenty of time for the trip. But through a series of delays, from stormy weather to multiple military roadblocks and a truck accident, we found ourselves in Nuevo Laredo, nearly thirteen hours later, as night was rapidly falling; we couldn't find our way to the international bridge. I was driving, Arlene navigating. She spotted a billboard with directions to the bridge. Unfortunately, the directions were a paragraph long and in Spanish (we later learned Arlene needed cataract surgery and was struggling to see clearly). We drove by the billboard several times before understanding it. With a glimmer of light left, we found the bridge, and its many lanes of cars. Signs above indicated which lane one should be in. As it turned out, we were in a lane at the far opposite end of our assigned lane, with no chance of adjusting our position. When it was our turn to cross the bridge, I apologized to the young guard for being in the wrong lane. We must have looked our pathetic best, because he assured me it was not a problem and asked where we needed to go. He politely directed us to our hotel and wished us good luck. We were going to need it.

The next morning, we realized our small Nissan Versa was straining like the *Mayflower* crossing the Atlantic in winter and, at times, even listing from the weight. That's when we began a daily morning routine of jettisoning items. During the course of our six-day trip, we left a trail of abandoned goods in our wake, much like 19th century pioneers traveling in overly-burdened covered wagons. The first to go was Duke's enormous bed; he wouldn't need it for the trip, because we always reserved a room with two Queen beds, one for us and one for him. We would buy our boy a new bed upon arrival in Oregon. We also left behind a step-ladder as well as items I can no longer recall and which we felt we didn't need or could easily replace. Do you really need a step-ladder on the road? It's not as if we'll be replacing light bulbs.

Later that second day, somewhere along an empty stretch of West Texas, Arlene was pulled over by the Highway Patrol. Uh-oh, that's not good, we thought. Even the cat meowed the word "shit."

The Highway Patrolwoman parked her car behind ours, strolled up to Arlene, touched the brim of her hat and said, "I pulled you over, ma'am, because you were speeding." Arlene asked how fast she was going and was told seventy-eight in a seventy zone. This was West Texas, the land of wide-open spaces. She could have been going one-hundred-and-seventy miles per hour without endangering any species. Still. Texas. The officer asked to see our car insurance. We had separate insurance policies for driving in Mexico and in the U.S. I began searching the glove compartment for the document but without much luck. To set context, we had many documents with us, including proof of pet vaccinations. I found the insurance for Mexico but not for the States. That's when we upped our game and unleashed our short-fused Bickersons'

routine, yelling back and forth. We eventually found the U.S. insurance policy and the officer, not wanting to add more fuel to the fire, let us go with a warning.

From that point on, our road trip was uneventful, until we had a flat tire. It was early on a Saturday morning, and I was driving. Half-way between the Arizona cities of Tucson and Phoenix, the car started pulling forcefully to the right. Bam. A tire blew. Traveling at 70 mph, I slowed down and pulled to the shoulder of the road. We had our car towed to the nearest tire store.

Arlene and I, along with Duke, rode with the driver while Sadie stayed in our car. Duke sat next to the driver, who had never seen a poodle that big. The driver kept looking over at Duke and shaking his head in amazement. Three hours later, we were back on the road. We spent one night in Las Vegas, where we ordered-in enough Chinese food to feed the Kardashians, assuming they do eat, and two nights in Reno, where we visited family. Less than a week after our arrival in Medford, we had signed the papers and received the keys to our latest house purchase.

Friends we had made in San Miguel and who were now living in nearby Ashland, Oregon, joined us for the first walk-through of our house. I opened the door to the detached garage and saw two bodies curled up inside on the hard pavement. I shut the door quickly and turned to my friend, "There are two bodies in there." Since past is prologue, the murder in our Portland condo flashed before me. I opened the door again, and the two bodies came to life: two embarrassed teenagers in need of a place to spend the night. They politely apologized and left.

And so began our latest chapter in Oregon. Not with a bang but a slumber.

A Run-in with the Amish

I was walking in downtown Portland, Oregon, on my way to meet a friend for lunch. Two men approached me from the other direction. It's as if I had called central casting and asked them to send me two twenty-something males, very Portlandish, Mutt and Jeff-types (but not too Mutty or too Jeffy), both should be wearing ragged jeans and backpacks, leather vests, and no shirts. Chest hair optional. Because it's Portland, both must have several piercings and tats, and they should be heavy smokers. As we passed each other, I overheard the short one, waving his cigarette in the air for emphasis, tell his tall friend: "That's when I had my run-in with the Amish." True story.

And that's what I like about writing humor. Ideas are everywhere. You can never run out of them. You really can't. Best of all, they're free.

Post-college my resume read like a good-grief of odd jobs: military journalist, medical librarian, college instructor, book packer, mill worker, business owner, technical writer, software documentation manager, marketing manager. If I could have thrown in gold prospector and hobo,

I would have been Jack London. Between and during those jobs, I always worked on creative projects, mostly writing and cartooning and, like many of you with an itch to create, all of it in my spare time.

While at work, in addition to my regular job, I'd also be doing what's known in the computer industry as "background processing," working out story problems in the garage of my mind and jotting them down so I wouldn't forget. If I happened to get mugged coming home from work, the unlucky guy would get scraps of paper and yellow Sticky Notes with bits of dialogue, plot points, and partly developed scenes on them. Not exactly stuff you can easily fence.

For three years, after hours, I even tried standup comedy to get over my shyness and really sucked at it—the standup part, not the shyness. Comedy bits about attending the Hemlock Society's Christmas Party ("Stay away from the punch"), and lines such as a linguistics professor at a bar hitting on a woman and saying, "Would you like to go up to my place and exchange bilabial fricatives?" did not exactly kill in biker bars. On the other hand, the tobacco smoke almost killed me.

One night a member of a successful Portland improv group complained to me that she couldn't write or tell jokes. In fact, she confessed to knowing only one joke and told it. She said: "I like my men like I like my ham—cured."

I thought it sounded more like a cheesy pickup line than a joke, and used it as a jumping off point for my first play.

When I was done writing it, I gave the play to my wife, Arlene, to read. She's always my first and most honest critic.

"This play is about dating," she said. "What the hell do you know about dating?"

Arlene was right, of course. My play was about dating, a topic I know nothing about.

Nonetheless, I continued writing plays, short plays befitting my height and attention span. As a part-time writer trying to squeeze in my words before going to work in the morning, late at night, or over the weekend in hourly chunks, I felt as if I never had enough time to tackle anything more substantial. I'm a Boomer. My gratification meter was stuck on Instant.

In the winter of 2001, I applied for and won a Walden Fellowship, which was awarded to three Oregon writers or artists each year. I accepted the fellowship, took an unpaid leave of absence from work, and spent six weeks during the spring of 2002 in a small cabin in the southern Oregon woods on an organic farm. The experience was liberating. For the first time in my life, my job, the entire point of my day, if you will, was to write whatever I wanted to write, eat when hungry, look for Bigfoot, and walk the dog. How cool was that?

After a few years of writing stage plays, I started writing screenplays. My first film script landed me a literary manager in L.A. and was a hot product for about 15 seconds. Someone at Maverick Films, at the time co-owned by Madonna and Guy Ritchie, loved the script and took it into studios, all of which passed. My second script was optioned by a production company but no movie was made. At least their check cleared the bank.

I like humor. Two of my literary heroes are the humorists Robert Benchley and James Thurber, while Mark Twain stands head and shoulders at the top of my Pantheon. And, if there are any Canadians out there reading these words, Stephen Leacock, who, along with Benchley pretty much invented the humorous essay as a literary form in the early 20th century, was also an influence. In more recent times, I've read and admired the humorous writings of Dave Barry, Woody Allen, David Sedaris, Steve Martin, Nora Ephron, Simon Rich, and many others.

Another favorite American humorist of mine is Jean Shepherd. I suspect most people know about him from the movie *A Christmas Story*, which is based on several of his stories about growing up in northwest Indiana in the 1940s. Shepherd shared his early years in two coming-of-age books: *Wanda Hickey's Night of Golden Memories: and Other Disasters* and *In God We Trust, All Others Pay Cash*. From reading Shepherd's books, I learned useful storytelling techniques and employed them in my first book. For example, I learned how to ease into and fill out a story, as well as how to drop-in pop-culture references.

I could have done a lot worse picking a memoir mentor. Jerry Seinfeld, for example, was a huge Jean Shepherd fan, as I later found out, and credited Shepherd with helping to form the famous Seinfeld comic perspective.

The simple truth is we all have stories. And to have a story that's worth sharing it isn't first necessary to have been locked in the Tower of London, suffered from toe fungus, discovered a cure for restless legs syndrome, or made a million dollars in the stock market by the time you were five. If you want to write your memoir, go for it. Even if you don't get everything right, don't worry. Charles Barkley, the former pro basketball star, once complained during a press conference that he had been misquoted in his autobiography. And *Seinfeld*, the enormously popular television show, according to one of its running gags, was about nothing.

In the preface to his classical yet whimsical autobiography, *My Life and Hard Times*, James Thurber said about humorists that the "little wheels of their invention are set in motion by the damp hand of melancholy."

It also helps, in my humble opinion, to have a run-in with the Amish, even if second-hand.

A Reader Asks

A reader of my memoir *Nobody Knows the Spanish I Speak* asked what I missed most about not living in the United States. Other readers asked different questions. I'm adding a few of their real questions and my answers below:

What did you miss most about not living in the United States?

Some cultures record their history by cataclysmic events: the year of the big fire or flood, the day the great earthquake or tornado struck. My history is recorded by my stomach. In conversations with my wife and friends, it's not unusual for me to interject a comment along the lines of, "Oh, I remember now, that was the time we were in San Francisco and I took my first bite of monkfish in lobster sauce." With such habits, it should come as no surprise that what I missed most about no longer living in the USA was Oregon's famous Dungeness crab.

San Miguel is in the middle of Mexico, six thousand feet up in the mountains and three thousand miles from the nearest Oregon crab pot. Oregon, it's been said, is like Ireland: All green and no gold. But if you ask me, there's plenty

of gold in Oregon, and it's usually panned in crabbing nets during winter.

I also still miss Trader Joe's, but who doesn't?

What cultural differences did you notice between Mexico and the U.S.?

We didn't get car-jacked, kidnapped, mistakenly shot at, or ripped off by a shady contractor hoping to live in Panama on our life savings.

But we had plenty of mishaps, made some dreadful mistakes, got in and out of trouble, and learned a thing or two about life, Mexico, and each other. Even though my memoir reenacts no homicides or rescue attempts, my story covers plenty of interesting ground, landscaped with prickly pear cactus, scorpions, mammoth speed bumps, lung-choking dust, yoga, disco, firecrackers, car repair, lost-in-translation moments, and a near-death collision on a highway in Mexico. All right, that last bit is an exaggeration. The six-wheeler missed us by a good five inches.

So, what was it like? We discovered we were living in a cash-based society where nobody ever had change.

In a culture where *mañana* did not always mean tomorrow but could mean anything from later to not now to fat chance you'll ever see me again.

In a country where the most common unit of measurement was not the kilo or the kilometer, as guidebooks would have you believe, but something known as *más o menos*, simply translated as "more or less." The people were kinder.

The pace was gentler. We felt like images on a postcard of San Miguel, surrounded daily as we were by streets made of cobblestones, brightly-colored houses, colonial-era churches, open-air street markets, and stoic burros laden with firewood. Enthusiastic street bands marched through town blissfully out of tune. Doctors made house calls; pharmacies delivered to our door.

And daily the sun appeared in all its resplendent glory, rarely blemished by dark clouds. The sun might not make a big difference if you come from, say, Arizona or Florida. But coming from the cloudy and damp Pacific Northwest, it was truly a sight to behold. It took us three days to figure out what that bright orb thing in the sky was, always looking down on us and making us feel happy and warm.

When you were little, what did you want to be when you "grew up"?

Tall. I like easy questions. Keep 'em coming.

How do you develop characters in your writing?

Plot, action, dialogue, conflict, scenes, descriptions, narration, exposition, and whatnot are all important elements of story, of course. But when I think of books I've read or movies I've watched, what most often sticks in my mind and stands tall are the characters, bad posture and all. I find such people, real or imaginary, hard to shake, and, for the most part, I don't want to shake them. In fact, I like having them sitting in the recesses of my recessed-hairline head, on

a bench, as if waiting for a bus to arrive or the coach to call their name ("Gatsby, in for Ahab. Now!").

Where were your main characters given life in the creative process?

Here we go. Another question about characters. It's not as if a writer can't create vivid and memorable characters when telling a true story. In fact, truth is quite often much stranger than fiction, as the saying goes, especially when it comes to people. One of my father's cousins, for example, had a hernia and would wear his truss outside of his pants. When writing a biography of a legend such as Marilyn Monroe, there is no shortage of interesting—and real—characters to introduce. But unless one has lived a rarified life, most of the people in one's own life are, well, not as interesting as, say Joe DiMaggio or Arthur Miller.

Throughout my memoir, I re-enforced our character traits, unassuming as they might be. For instance, I talked about how our driving skills complemented each other. I refused to ask for directions, and Arlene had absolutely no sense of direction at all. Stubborn is not a good character trait.

By the end of the book, if I have done my job correctly, the reader should feel as if he or she knows me and my wife and may choose to ignore us at parties or run the other way. We won't take it personally. Our pets might but we won't.

Why did you choose this setting?

Great question. Truth be told, I didn't choose the setting.

It's not as if I went to IKEA and picked out one of their small fully decorated rooms. But I get what you're saying. It doesn't matter if it's about a fish out of water, a stranger in a strange land, or landing a strange fish, all such stories are largely about setting. Shortly after the story opens, if not at its very beginning, the central character is thrown into an unfamiliar milieu and events—good and bad—take place. The story is off and running. Yadda-yadda-yadda. Badda bing, badda boom. The end.

In our case, the first time we lived in San Miguel, during the period covered in my memoir, we lived in *La Lejona*, a mostly Mexican middleclass neighborhood with wide, cobbled or unpaved streets, dust everywhere except during the rainy season, and an impressive backdrop of cacti and mountains. *La Lejona* is the kind of Mexican neighborhood where foreigners pat themselves on the back for living among the locals while Mexicans pat themselves on the back for living among foreigners. Our neighborhood was less than a thirty-minute walk, mostly flat, into the popular historic *Centro*, a fifteen-minute bus ride, ten minutes by car or taxi, and mere seconds by a Star Trek transporter. The second time we lived in San Miguel, we moved to a neighborhood closer in to the center of town and sold the transporter.

If you were a superhero what would your name be?

Karma Cop. Theme music plays in the background; a commanding voice speaks over a montage of scenes showing yours truly in action: "He's a loose cannon on the Road

to Enlightenment, making the world safe for truth, justice, and the cosmic way." As Karma Cop, I would make sure what goes around comes around. Best of all, I'd get to wear a cape.

So how was the issue of racism in Mexico? Sort of a tables turned question. Did you experience any resentment because you're an American living in their country? I am curious.

As a stranger in a strange land, it is easy to be taken advantage of and easier still to be discriminated against. However, like Blanche Dubois, I have always depended on the kindness of strangers. And kind they have been.

My wife and I have been invited to large Mexican weddings, as well as to intimate dinners at Mexican houses. Neighbors smile gently and correct me when I butcher their language, even though a simple word such as "*huevos*" can have two meanings, one of which is guaranteed to get you in trouble. When my wife fell on the street one afternoon, a Mexican man rushed out from his office to help her up and make sure she was okay. When we pulled over to the side of the street because of a flat tire, a man ran across the street and a cab driver pulled in behind us, both offering to help. These are anecdotes and, of course, I could go on.

Restaurant waiters still wait on me. Cab drivers don't ignore me because I'm not one of them. And I have yet to find a mob of Mexicans outside my door late at night, waving torches, and shouting, "Yankee, Go Home."

Where do you get your ideas?

I think the real question should be: Where do you not get ideas? Henry James said if you want to be a writer, "Try to be one of the people on whom nothing is lost!" So, that's where you get your ideas. Everywhere. Don't lose a thing. It's all usable.

For example, "Oedipus and Hamlet Walk into a Bar" is the name of a short play I wrote several years ago. It was based on the title of a workshop I was asked to give as a gag cartoonist to playwrights about humor, designed to be part of a planned writers' weekend, which never happened. Instead, I took the title and wrote a play around it, the only time, for me anyway, in which the title came first. I didn't have a play in mind or knew what to write until I realized that both "Ed" and "Ham" had mommy issues. Bingo. I took two of the most tragic male figures in Western literature and found humor by putting them together in a modern-day bar sipping long-neck beers, where Ed (Oedipus) tells Ham (Hamlet) he thinks Ham's mom is hot.

All writers have favorite quotes. What's yours?

"Dr. Seuss, you have an imagination with a long tail." (from a child's letter to Ted Geisel).

Afterword

Arlene and I first saw San Miguel de Allende during a U.S. holiday weekend, President's Day, in February of 2005. We spent most of that vacation in the city of Guanajuato, an hour's drive west of San Miguel. We visited San Miguel only once during that time and for less than two hours. Arlene and two friends toured the *Centro* historic district; I accompanied two other friends to Harry's (now known as Hank's) for beef sliders and a cold beer.

We decided after that brief vacation to follow our bliss, as Joseph Campbell urged, and, as advised earlier by Henry James, to live the life we had imagined. We returned to Portland, Oregon, left our jobs, dropped out, sold most of our possessions, and moved—lock, stock, and pets—to San Miguel. That was the first move.

The second time we moved to San Miguel, we had returned to Portland and lived there for three years before heading south again. The third time, aka our most recent move, we left southern Oregon, where we had made our home for four years in the beautiful Rogue River Valley, and returned to San Miguel. Since 2005, we've lived in San

Miguel as full-time residents for eight of the last 15 years. We consider it home. Finally. Maybe. We hope.

In 2006, during our initial period of life in San Miguel, I was watching a U.S. business news program. Some cocky young blonde guy, a frat boy in a three-piece suit, snidely commented that Mexico had a siesta economy: any time the sun comes out they take a siesta. I wanted to punch that jerk in his flabby face. In my experience, nobody works harder than the average Mexican. Not only that, they are incredibly entrepreneurial. More recently, mere weeks ago, in fact, from the time I write these words, I watched in disgust a video clip on the internet as an ignorant, angry American white male verbally assaulted a young man because the young man was talking to his mother in Spanish in the waiting area of a U.S. airport. First, it was a private conversation. Second, whenever Arlene and I traveled, say to Europe, we only spoke English to each other in private conversation. As the blues standard goes, "Ain't nobody's business if I do."

What's wrong with these people in the United States? Besides the fact that many of them can barely speak their own language, I suspect they've never visited another country. What a sad loss for them to see their world as so small it only includes those who look and talk the way they do.

The U.S. is a multi-racial country, regardless of what some knuckle draggers in red baseball caps might think. A check on the percentage of races in the USA can be enlightening. The number one race of origin is German at slightly under 15%. After that, it's non-Hispanic Black or African

American at slightly over 12%. In third is Mexican, at nearly 11%, followed closely behind by Irish. Twenty-one percent of the population, or roughly 61 million people, speak a language other than English (as their first language). Spanish tops the list as the most frequently spoken non-English language in the United States, accounting for 62 percent of all foreign language speakers, or a total of 38 million people.

During our second residency in San Miguel, we attended a New Year's Eve dinner party at a nearby restaurant. The dining room was on the second floor, giving us a view of the city. At midnight, everyone dining in the restaurant went outside to the balcony to watch, as a relentless batch of fireworks brightened the dark sky, backed up by noise loud enough to make you believe it was made of solid matter instead of unseen vibrations. We wished each other Happy New Year, clinked glasses, and drank our champagne.

Another diner, a well-dressed Mexican man who was there celebrating with friends, offered a second toast. In clear English, he toasted the Americans and Canadians in the room and thanked them for still believing in Mexico.

About the Author

Mark Saunders is a former winner of the Walden Fellowship, awarded to only three Oregon writers or artists each year. Back in his drawing days, more than 500 of his cartoons were published nationally, in publications as diverse as *The San Jose Mercury News*, *Writer's Digest*, *The Saturday Evening Post*, and *Twilight Zone Magazine*.

As a freelance gag writer, he sold jokes to standup comics, including Jay Leno, and wrote for the highly successful "Frank and Ernest" comic strip. Mark's feature screenplays include "The Big Sheep" (co-author); "Hotel Manana" (co-author); "Worst Friends Forever" (co-author); "Manana" (sole author); "Pinot Gris and Curly Fries" (sole author); "Team Poodle" (sole author, optioned twice); "Two Weeks in Roswell" (sole author, optioned twice); and "Yo, Nostradamus" (sole author). His film scripts have won awards.

Mark's stage plays have been performed in the U.S., Mexico, and England. Five of his act-one plays ("Who's on Faust?"; "Playthings"; "Some People Say"; "Two People"; "Fictionistas") have been published by Smith and Kraus, along with two of his monologues (from the plays "Am I Right?"

and “The Line Forms in My Rear”). His essays have appeared in Volumes I, II, and III of *Solamente en San Miguel*, as well as in online publications.

Mark’s humorous award-winning memoir about dropping out and moving to Mexico, *Nobody Knows the Spanish I Speak*, was originally published by Fuze Publishing (www.fuzepublishing) and may now be ordered from their website, bookstores or Amazon, as well as from the Knish Books website (www.knishbooks.com). *Dogs, Cats & Expats* is his second book.

Mark once owned a Yugo (please don’t ask about the car).

Nobody Knows the Spanish I Speak

An Excerpt

A month before leaving for Mexico, we were safely ensconced in our Portland condo seven floors above the insects. I was obsessing loudly about scorpions. In thinking back, I envisioned myself in full Napoleonic regalia, pacing from one end of the room to the other, a worried scowl on my face, hands clasped behind my back. Clearly, war loomed on the horizon.

"You're fixating on scorpions," Arlene said. "They're probably not as dangerous as you think."

"Hmm," I said.

Arlene believes the whole point of evolution was to get off the ground and sleep on clean linen in comfortable hotels. She might be right, but she's also an equal-opportunity bug hater and treats a ladybug with the same disdain as she does a black widow spider. She knew even less about scorpions than I did.

"Why don't you Google them to see what you can find out?" she added.

"Good idea. A little knowledge is a dangerous thing," I replied.

I knew she was right. I needed to do more research. Soon we would be living in Mexico, and by then it would be too late. Besides, it couldn't be as bad as my imagination let on.

It wasn't as bad. It was worse.

Excerpt from "Scorpions Ascendant" a chapter in *Nobody Knows the Spanish I Speak,* voted a Top 3 book in San Miguel.

Knish Books

Our focus as Knish Books is in two general areas of interest: food writing and humor writing. Or, as we like to say, food that makes you smile and laughs that make you hungry. As publishers, we are both writers who spent many years in the business world working as technical and marketing communicators and now, in retirement, enjoy sharing our experiences about food, life, love, and fantasy football.

www.ingramcontent.com/pod-product-compliance
Lightning Source LLC
LaVergne TN
LVHW091054080826
845145LV00002B/743

9781737515500